Dynamics of
POVERTY ALLEVIATION PROGRAMMES

Dynamics of POVERTY ALLEVIATION PROGRAMMES

AJIT KUMAR SINHA
D.Litt.
Pro-Vice Chancellor
T.M. Bhagalpur University, Bhagalpur

DEEP & DEEP PUBLICATIONS PVT. LTD.
F-159, Rajouri Garden, New Delhi-110027

ISBN 81-7629-387-3

Typeset by S.S. COMPOSERS,
3190, Mohindra Park, Shakur Basti, Delhi-110034.

Printed in India at ELEGANT PRINTERS,
A-38/2, Maya Puri, Phase-I, New Delhi-110064.

Published by DEEP & DEEP PUBLICATIONS PVT. LTD.,
F-159, Rajouri Garden, New Delhi-110027.
Phones: 5435369, 5440916

CONTENTS

PREFACE

Abject poverty exposes the hollowness of our system. Teeming poverty with the developed nuclear power is not only a paradox of our time but a shame for the civil society of the 21st century. Alleviation of poverty has been the goal of our development strategy since the beginning. Initially efforts were made to alleviate poverty with trickle-down hypothesis of the mainstream of development efforts. The strategy has been supplemented/complemented with the policy of direct attack on poverty since late 1970s.

The most unfortunate aspect is that even the combined strategy could not achieve any significant result and the actual number of poor has risen. The regional variation in the poverty level is an added dimension of the dilemma. Bihar (undivided) represents the poorest among the poor.

A survey has been conducted on 752 selected beneficiaries of different poverty alleviation programmes from three selected zones, i.e., North Bihar, Central Bihar and Jharkhand to evaluate the efficacy of the policy of direct attack on poverty.

The report is divided into six chapters. An introduction in Chapter 1 contains the description of problem, methodology and the Socio-economic condition of the beneficiaries as a whole in general and North Bihar, Central Bihar and Jharkhand in particular. This is followed by the evaluation of Self-Employment Programmes including IRDP, TRYSEM and DWCRA in Chapter 2. Chapter 3 has highlighted the Wage Employment Programmes including JRY and EAS. IAY has been evaluated in Chapter 4. Chapter 5 has evaluated the National Social Assistance Programme which includes NOAPS, NFBS and NMBS. Broad conclusion has been presented in Chapter 6.

The survey has shown that a sizeable proportion of beneficiaries have income either above poverty line or in the upper income-slab below poverty line. Most of the anti-poverty schemes have been implemented on paper and the scarce financial resources have been grossly misutilised under the influence of the Crime-Syndicates and the speed money. Common masses are unaware and trivial about the programmes. Structural transformation is needed for a qualitative break in the system.

In preparation of this book, I have received unqualified co-operation and assistance from a multitude of personalities and institutions to all of whom I owe a personal debt.

First of all I wish to record my gratitude to the Planning Commission, New Delhi for selection of the project and giving the opportunity.

I am immensely thankful to Md. Tarique for calculation of the poverty indices; Dr. Amrendra for preparing the schedules etc., Mr. M.P. Roy, Dr. Subodh Kumar Sinha and Dr. Kalyani for day-to-day co-operation and Mr. Rakesh Raman, Mr. N.K. Singh and Dr. R.V.P. Singh for their valuable suggestions.

I am extremely thankful to Dr. C.K.P. Shahi for his valuable advice in the survey methodology.

I am also thankful to Dr. Jitendra Sharma, Mr. Manoj Kumar, Mr. Ashok K. Mishra, Mr. Saket B. Singh, Smt. Rita Kumari and Mr. Shailendra Choudhary for their tireless efforts in the process of field investigation.

I am specially thankful to Mr. Nemai Pal for data analysis and management and Mr. K.K. Sahu for preparation of figures and Mr. Mukesh Kumar and his Vandana Computers for typing the manuscripts.

The concerned block authorities of Katra (Distt. Muzaffarpur), Nagar Nausha (Distt. Nalanda) and Barhait (Distt. Sahibganj) and the Bank authorities of Union Bank of India, Katra Branch (Distt. Muzaffarpur) Punjab National Bank, Khirubigha Branch (Distt. Nalanda), State Bank of India, Barhait Branch (Distt. Sahibganj) deserve special thanks for their valuable co-operation in the process of field investigation.

I shall be failing in my duty if I do not express my gratefulness to all those who have helped our field investigators during the survey in various ways.

It is my pleasure and privilege to thank all those who have contributed directly and indirectly to the study.

AJIT KUMAR SINHA

EXECUTIVE SUMMARY

Poverty alleviation has been the basic goal of our plans since the beginning of the plan era. Earlier the plan models had visualized that the Trickle Down Effect would result in higher income opportunities for the poor sector and significant dent on the incidence of poverty. A distinct change in the strategy of poverty alleviation was visualized since later part of 1970s. Instead of relying on growth to percolate, efforts were initiated to directly attack the problem of poverty by endowing the poor with productive asset/skill to employ themselves to earn larger income. Policy initiatives were also taken to create additional opportunities for wage employment essentially as a supplement to fill the gaps of unemployment in the lean seasons. A number of poverty alleviation measures were introduced in the 6th five year plan and the subsequent plans followed suit.

The report based on sample survey of 752 beneficiaries from poverty alleviation programmes of North Bihar, Central Bihar and Jharkhand has evaluated the efficacy of poverty alleviation programmes.

The overview and methodology of the study have been presented in the introductory chapter. The chapter has also assessed the socio-economic condition of the beneficiaries with the help of different poverty indices. Chapter 2 has evaluated the efficacy of the programmes of self-employment including IRDP (now SGSY), TRYSEM and DWCRA. Chapter 3 has evaluated the efficacy of wage employment programmes—JRY and EAS. Chapter 4 deals with the Indira Awaas Yojana (IAY). Chapter 5 focusses on National Social Assistance Programmes including NOAPS, NFBS and NMBS. A broad conclusion and policy recommendation of the study have been presented in Chapter 6.

The study has confirmed that the poverty alleviation programmes have not made any significant dent on the problem of poverty. Poverty of poverty alleviation programmes jointly with anti-development institutional framework have successfully kept the poverty intact. The abject poverty is prevalent over the system in tune with the global counterparts with the following characteristics :

1. Lack of income and assets to attain basic necessities—food, shelter, clothing and acceptable level of health and education.
2. Sense of voicelessness and powerlessness in the institutions of state and society.
3. Vulnerability to adverse shocks, linked to an inability to cope with them.

Broad Findings

(i) 24.0% beneficiaries of poverty alleviation programmes have income above poverty line, despite that they have taken the benefit of the schemes through their manipulating skills.

(ii) A large proportion of beneficiaries are in the upper income-slab below poverty line in all the survey zones and schemes. Sen-Index has confirmed it in case of the zones and the schemes earlier.

(iii) Poverty alleviation schemes have been implemented only on paper to misutilise the resources in significant proportion.

(iv) All the poverty alleviation schemes in all the zones have been deeply influenced by payment of speed money. In other words, the payment of speed money has been an essential condition for getting the benefit of anti-poverty schemes with few exceptions.

(v) Neither the authorities nor the beneficiaries have taken the schemes in their true spirit. The authorities have taken it as a source of additional resource mobilisation for their own and subject to complete mere formalities. The beneficiaries have taken the assistance as a subsidy without any serious thought on the purpose of the assistance and the possibilities.

(vi) No system could be evolved for mass awareness about the poverty alleviation schemes. The amount received under the scheme have been siphoned off in collaboration with the concerned authorities and the local power brokers/middlemen due to unawareness of the common masses.

Poverty alleviation schemes have been implemented in the form of distribution of alms without any serious consideration to generate viable income or service.

(vii) Procedural delay/bureaucratic red-tapism has been a common feature in execution of poverty alleviation programmes.

(viii) NGOs and PRIs have played no role in the implementation of poverty alleviation schemes. PRIs have been completely defunct in the state as no election was held in between 1978 and 2000.

Schemes for direct attack on poverty were introduced to supplement/complement the mainstream of development effort under the *trickle-down hypothesis*. Slow rate of growth of the economy alongwith maintained population growth rate had necessitated to go for direct attack on poverty. But the empirical evaluation of the poverty alleviation programmes, i.e., direct attack on poverty reveals that the significant proportion of the schemes had been misutilised in the name of poverty alleviation. Abject poverty has been considered as a good politics and scarce resources were wasted mercilessly without reaching the poor.

Policy Recommendations

Poverty cannot be alleviated in a fragmented cartesian manner. A holistic approach is required to break the Neo vicious circle of poverty. Half-hearted, faltering and piece-meal efforts may be a good politics but a bad economics. In this background the following recommendations are propounded for a structural transformation of the system :

(i) Schemes must have viable income generating potentials. Without consideration of viable income, no scheme should be undertaken to misuse the scarce resources.

(ii) Transparent and time-bound implementation procedure should be evolved and tendency of concerned authorities and power brokers to siphon-off the funds of the schemes should be effectively curbed.

(iii) Without raising the honest and efficient administrative level no qualitative break would be possible in the system. A viable policy for the metamorphosis of the economic administration should be evolved.

(iv) Resources should be allocated for primary education specially for job-oriented education which would generate maximum total linkage effect in the system.

(v) Health facilities should be improved and special attention should be given on family-based welfare measure to reduce the population pressure.

(vi) NGOs should be assigned dynamic role in the process of poverty alleviation specially in the field of mass education and mass awareness.

(vii) Effective decentralized system should be strengthened by making the Panchayati Raj Institutions (PRIs) functional.

(viii) Pragmatic decision should be taken to salvage the system from the traps of Crime-Syndicates functioning in perfect nexus with bureaucracy, policy, politicians and mafias to siphon off any type of resources with chickenery methods.

(ix) Lastly, the recommendation of the Independent South Asian Commission on Poverty Alleviation should be implemented in the form of Sociogram to break the Neo Vicious Circle of Poverty (i.e., Vicious Circle of Poverty under institutional framework) and initiate the virtuous circle of development.

ABBREVIATIONS

B.D.O.	:	Block Development Officer
B.P.L.	:	Below Poverty Line
D.R.D.A	:	District Rural Development Authority
D.W.C.R.A	:	Development of Women & Children in Rural Areas
E.A.S.	:	Employment Assurance Scheme
G.K.Y.	:	Ganga Kalyan Yojana
H.C.I.	:	Head-Count Index
H.P.I.	:	Human Poverty Index
I.A.Y	:	Indira Awaas Yojana
I.G.R.	:	Income Gap Ratio
I.R.D.P.	:	Integrated Rural Development Programme
J.G.S.Y.	:	Jawahar Gram Samriddhi Yojana
J.R.Y.	:	Jawahar Rozgar Yojana
M.F.	:	Marginal Farmer
M.W.S.	:	Millions Well Scheme
N.F.B.S.	:	National Family Benefit Scheme
N.G.O.	:	Non-Governmental Organisation
N.M.B.S.	:	National Maternity Benefit Scheme
N.O.A.P.S.	:	National Old Age Pension Scheme
N.R.E.P.	:	National Rural Employment Programme

N.S.A.P.	:	National Social Assistance Programme
O.B.C.	:	Other Backward Class
P.D.S.	:	Public Distribution System
P.G.I.	:	Poverty Gap Index
P.P.P.	:	Purchasing Power Parity
P.R.Is.	:	Panchayati Raj Institutions
R.L.E.G.P.	:	Rural Landless Employment Guarantee Programme
S.C.	:	Scheduled Caste
S.F.	:	Small Farmer
S.G.S.Y.	:	Swarnajayanti Gram Swarojgar Yojana
S.H.Gs.	:	Self-Help Groups
S.I.T.RA.	:	Supply of Improved Toolkits to Rural Artisans
S.P.G.I.	:	Squared Poverty Gap Index
S.T.	:	Scheduled Tribe
T.R.Y.S.E.M.	:	Training of Rural Youth for Self-employment
U.T.	:	Union Territory
V.L.W.	:	Village Level Worker

CHAPTER

1

INTRODUCTION

OVERVIEW

The process of sustainable development must bring the degree of abject poverty to a minimum level as far as possible. The relative poverty is a universal fact and has existed in every society at all times. The matter of serious contemporary concern is, a maintained level of abject poverty of the exposed poor masses, deprived of basic human needs under the Glass Curtain Economy. The process of sustainable development is badly obstructed by the Neo Vicious Circle of Poverty which implies a circular constellation of forces tending to act and react upon one another in such a way as to keep a poor country in a state of poverty. It is a humiliating reality before the civil society and world's greatest challenge of the 21st century.

South Asia has been the centre of poverty. Out of 1.2 billion developing world's poor (20% of the total population living on less than $1 a day), 43.5 percent live in South Asia (India, Pakistan, Bangladesh, Nepal, Bhutan, Maldives, Sri Lanka and Afganistan), 24.3 percent in Sub-saharan Africa, 23.2 percent in East Asia and Pacific, 6.5 percent in Latin America and Carribean, 2.0 percent in Europe and Central Asia and 0.5 percent in the Middle East and North Africa. (Annex 1 & 2).

The poverty has resulted into low survival rate; low adult literacy rate; population without access to safe water, health services and sanitation and under weight children below the age of five amongst the poor in the developing world (Annex 3).

Poverty has been historically identified as the main persistent malady of the Indian Economy. Calculations of poverty indices for the Indian economy including Head-Count Index (HCI), Poverty Gap Index (PGI) and Squared Poverty Gap Index (SPGI) from August 1951 to December 1997 have clearly revealed that poverty had persisted in our system in a chequered way and the absolute number of poor has risen (Annex 4).

State wise variation in poverty level is an added dimension of the problem. Undivided Bihar had the highest poverty level from all the three poverty estimates i.e. HCI, PGI and SPGI. The classified estimation for rural and urban poverty indicate that rural poverty was the highest in Bihar, but this place was occupied by Madhya Pradesh in case of urban poverty (Annex 5). Since 74.29% & 86.86% poor live in rural areas in India and Bihar respectively, the rural setting has a predominant impact on the poverty situation.

Bihar had been at the top of the poverty-striken states of the country. But poverty indices for different zones of different states reveal that the poverty level of Madhya Pradesh South/West, Orissa South, and UP South was higher in comparison to all the three zones of undivided Bihar. Himalayan region of West Bengal, Maharastra Inland Central and Maharashtra Inland East had higher poverty than Central Bihar. But poverty in all the three zones of undivided Bihar was higher in comparison to the remaining zones of the different states of the country. North Bihar had been the poorest region of undivided Bihar followed by Jharkhand. Central Bihar had been better placed (Annex 6).

POVERTY ALLEVIATION

Reduction in poverty and unemployment and improvement in the quality of life have been the basic goals of our plans which have remained unchanged since the beginning of the plan era. The earlier Indian plan models had visualised that the *Trickle Down effect* would result in higher income opportunities for the poor sector and significant dent on the incidence of poverty. But the average annual growth rate was around 3.5 percent against the desired growth rate of 5.0 percent during the first three decades of planning and the growth rate of population could not be brought down which jointly resulted extremely low per capita income growth and exposed the trickle down hypothesis.

A distinct change in the strategy of poverty alleviation was visualised since later part of 1970s. Instead of relying on growth to percolate, efforts were initiated to directly attack the problem of poverty by endowing the poor with productive assets/skill to employ themselves to earn larger income. Policy initiatives were also taken to create additional opportunities for wage employment essentially as a supplement to fill the gaps of unemployment in lean seasons. A number of poverty alleviation measures were introduced in the Sixth Five Year Plan and the subsequent Plans followed suit.

THE SURVEY

The study has evaluated the efficacy of the poverty alleviation programmes on the basis of data collected from the sample survey of 752 beneficiaries from poverty alleviation programmes of North Bihar, Central Bihar and Jharkhand (now the separate state) applying the structural-functional method. (Tables 1.0 - 1.3)

Bihar was divided into three above mentioned geographical regions since the separation of Orissa in 1935. The entire poverty alleviation programmes under the plans have been implemented on the uniform basis in all the three regions till creation of separate Jharkhand state bifurcated from Bihar on 15th November, 2000.

The survey was conducted in between April-September, 2000. Hence, one unit from each zone was selected to make the study representatives. Units have been selected on the basis of multistage sampling method.

One district from each zone was selected on a random basis. From each selected district only a single block was taken up on the same basis and from each block village Panchayats were selected for sample collection as unit areas. The village panchayats have been taken as units for the sample survey because villages are usually found to be too small to serve as an

TABLE 1.0

Scheme-wise Distribution of Beneficiaries

Zone	*Self-Employment Programmes*			*Wage-Employment Programmes*		*National Housing Scheme*	*National Social Assistance Programmes*			*Total*
	IRDP	*TRYSEM*	*DWCRA*	*JRY*	*EAS*	*IAY*	*NOAPS*	*NFBS*	*NMBS*	
North Bihar	60	20	20	60	20	20	20	09	20	249
Central Bihar	60	20	20	60	20	20	20	03	20	243
Jharkhand	60	20	20	60	20	20	20	20	20	260
Total	180	60	60	180	60	60	60	32	60	752

TABLE : 1.1

Categorisation of Beneficiaries

Zone	*Sex*		*Literacy*		*Literacy Level*			*Beneficiary's Occupation at the Time of Selection*						
	Male	*Female*	*Literate*	*Illiterate*	*Primary & above*	*Matric & above*	*Graduation & above*	*SF*	*MF*	*Agri-Labour*	*Non-agri. Casual Labour*	*Non-agri. Self employed*	*Artisan*	*Others*
North Bihar	176	73	82	167	67	14	01	7	01	132	16	60	01	32
Central Bihar	150	93	121	122	70	43	08	32	35	104	12	39	17	04
Jharkhand	171	89	169	91	129	34	06	21	01	27	82	95	05	29
Total	497	255	372	380	266	91	15	60	37	263	110	194	23	65

TABLE 1.2

Size of the Family and Social Classification

Zone	*Size of the Family*			*Social Classification*						
				Category I				*Category II*		
	1-5	*6-11*	*12+*	*SC*	*ST*	*OBCs*	*Others*	*Ex/freed bonded labour*	*Assignies of surplus land*	*Others*
North Bihar	93	149	07	141	00	69	39	00	07	242
Central Bihar	109	120	14	146	00	96	01	22	00	221
Jharkhand	129	130	01	31	10	211	08	00	03	257
Total	331	399	22	318	10	376	48	22	10	720

TABLE 1.3

Family Income

Zone	Below Poverty Line			Above Poverty Line		
	Upto 6400	6401-11000	11001-16000	16001-21000	21001-32000	32001+
North Bihar	04	14	74	78	60	19
Central Bihar	06	20	60	79	40	38
Jharkhand	12	46	92	78	31	01
Total	22	80	226	235	131	58

adequate area unit. The selected districts are Muzaffarpur from North Bihar, Nalanda from Central Bihar and Sahebganj from Jharkhand and the selected blocks are Katra in Muzaffarpur, Nagar Nausha in Nalanda and Barhait in Sahebganj.

Katra Panchayat of Katra block in Muzaffarpur was selected for the sample survey. As adequate number of beneficiaries were not available in the Katra block, the remaining targetted samples were collected from the adjacent village Panchayats including Gangeya, Dhanaur and Tehawara. The sample survey collected from the villages are namely Katra, Deogan, Sonepur, Bakhri, Shiswara, Gotoli, Banjari in Katra Panchayat and Nawada, Madhopur, Bhawanipur and Barri village in Gangeya Panchayat, Rajadih and Sakri Village in Dhanaur Panchayat and Tehawara village in Tehawara Panchayat.

Vishnupur-Daldali chowk Panchayat of Nagar Nausha block in the district of Nalanda in Central Bihar was selected for the sample survey. But as adequate number of beneficiaries were not available in Nagar Nansha block, the remaining targetted samples were collected from the adjacent Korari Panchayat. The samples collected from the villages are namely Khansaria, Lachchubigha, Khirubigha, Hajipur, Bajetpur, Khazura, Daldalichak, Fauzdaribigha, Vishnupur, Shivalayapur and Sakarpura, Chainpura, Panchrukhiya, Mahanandapur, Bodhibigha in Vishnupur-Daldalichak Panchayat, Mustafapur and Chakmunni villages in Korari Panchayat.

Barhait Panchayat of Barhait block in the district of

Sahebganj in Jharkhand region was selected for sample survey. Adequate number of beneficiaries was available in the Barhait block. The samples collected from the villages are namely Barhait Santhali, Sonajori, Dhanjori and Barhait Bazar in the Barhait Panchayat.

Beneficiaries from 35 villages-14 from North Bihar, 17 from Central Bihar and 4 from Jharkhand were surveyed. IRDP was the oldest and most important on-going poverty alleviation programme under the self-employed scheme. Hence, 180 samples-60 from each zone were collected from the beneficiaries of the IRDP. The other important poverty alleviation programmes under self-employed programmes are TRYSEM and DWCRA. Till 1991 TRYSEM was part of IRDP main programme. DWCRA came into existence since 1982-83. 60 samples - 20 from each zone were selected from the TRYSEM beneficiaries and similar number of beneficiaries were surveyed i.e., 20 from each zone from the DWCRA beneficiaries. The Govt. of India has launched Supply of Improved Toolkits to Rural Artisans (SITRA) scheme since July 1992 with a financial ceiling of Rs. 2,000 for improved hand tools. The beneficiaries have to pay only 10% of the amount and the remaining 90% would be subsidy. But the ceiling for power driven tools is Rs. 4500. The scheme was not in the knowledge of the common men of all the three zones and the block authorities could not supply the list of beneficiaries of the scheme. Hence, no sample could be collected from the beneficiaries of the scheme.

JRY was the oldest and most important on-going scheme under wage employment programmes. 180 samples - 60 from each zone were selected from the beneficiaries of JRY. The 2nd wage employment programme - EAS was launched on 2nd October, 1999 in drought prone desert, tribal and hilly areas. But with the merger of 722 blocks covered under the 2nd stream of JRY the EAS had been universalised with effect from April, 1997. 60 samples - 20 from each zone were taken from the beneficiaries of the scheme. The Government of India had given a separate status to the Million Wells Scheme (MWS) with effect from January, 1996 to provide open irrigation wells to the target groups. But surprisingly block authorities had shown complete ignorance about the scheme and could not supply the list of the beneficiaries. Hence, the scheme could not be evaluated under the study. Indira Awaas Yojna IAY had received separate status with effect from January, 1996 after restructuring of the JRY. 60 samples - 20 from each zone were taken from the beneficiaries of the scheme.

National Social Assistance Programme (NSAP) came into existence from August 15, 1995 for social assistance to the poor households in case of old age death of primary bread winner and maternity with 100% Central assistance. The scheme has three components - NMBS, NFBS and NOAPS. 60 samples - 20 from each zone were selected from the beneficiaries of NOAPS and the same number of samples were selected from the beneficiaries of NMBS. But only 32 samples could be collected from the beneficiaries of NFBS. 20 beneficiaries of the scheme were surveyed at Jharkhand but only 9 beneficiaries of the scheme could be surveyed at North Bihar and only 3 at the Central Bihar as adequate number of beneficiaries were not available in the selected village panchayats and their adjoining areas.

The samples had been collected out of beneficiaries' list supplied by the block and bank authorities of the concerned block on the basis of linear systematic procedure and the stratified sampling method. Specifically prepared schedules had been used for the survey of beneficiaries of different schemes/ Programmes.

To verify the various observations made during the survey by the beneficiaries, some interviews were taken from the block authorities, bank authorities, DRDA authorities, Gram Sevaks, VLWs and prominent social workers.

Limitations of the Study

The study had not evaluated land reforms and Public Distribution system (PDS) and Urban-poverty Alleviation Programmes due to vast and complex nature with countless dimensions. They deserve separate study. It was not possible to cover them under one umbrella.

SOCIO-ECONOMIC CONDITION OF THE BENEFICIARIES

752 beneficiaries were surveyed under the study to evaluate the performance of poverty alleviation programmes

under the scheme - Direct Attack On Poverty. The data had been collected in similar proportion form North Bihar, Central Bihar and Jharkhand except for NFBS. 497 (66.09%) beneficiaries were male and 255 (33.91%) were female. 372 (49.5%) beneficiaries were literate and 380 (50.50%) were illiterate. Out of 372 literate population 266 (35.37%) had only primary education i.e., below matriculation, 91 (12.10%) had secondary and senior secondary education, only 15 (2.0%) had graduation and above qualification. (Charts 1 & 2)

60 (7.97%) beneficiaries were small farmers, 37 (4.92%) were marginal farmers, 263 (34.97%) were agricultural labourers, 110 (14.62%) were non-agricultural casual labourers, 194 (25.79%) were non-agricultural self-employed, 23 (3.05%) were artisans and 65 (8.64%) were others including housewives.

331 (44.01%) beneficiaries had a family size of 1-5 members, 339 (45.07%) had a family size of 6-11 members, only 22 (2.93%) had a family size of 12 or more i.e., combined family. (Charts 3 & 4)

318 (42.28%) beneficiaries were schedule castes, 10 (1.39%) were scheduled tribes, 376 (50.0%) were OBCs and 48 (6.38%) belonged to others including minorities. Only 22 (2.92%) beneficiaries were ex/freed bonded labourers and 10 (1.39%) were assignees of surplus land. Remaining 720 (95.74%) beneficiaries were of others/general categories. (Charts 5 & 6)

Poverty Line

Following the recommendations of The Task Force On Minimum Needs And Effective Consumption Demand (1979) the planning commission has been estimating the proportion and the number of poor separately for rural and urban India at National as well as State levels. The estimates have been released from the year 1972-73 onwards, using the full survey data on household consumption expenditure collected by NSSO at different intervals. The Official estimate is based on a calorie norm of 2400 calories per capita per day for rural areas and 2100 calories per capita per day for urban areas. The Task Force (1979) defined the poverty line equivalent to Rs. 49.09 and Rs. 56.64 per capita per month for rural and urban areas respectively at 1973-74 prices.

The poverty line has been updated from time to time

CHART 1

Categorisation of Beneficiaries of Poverty Alleviation Progarmmes

Sex Ratio

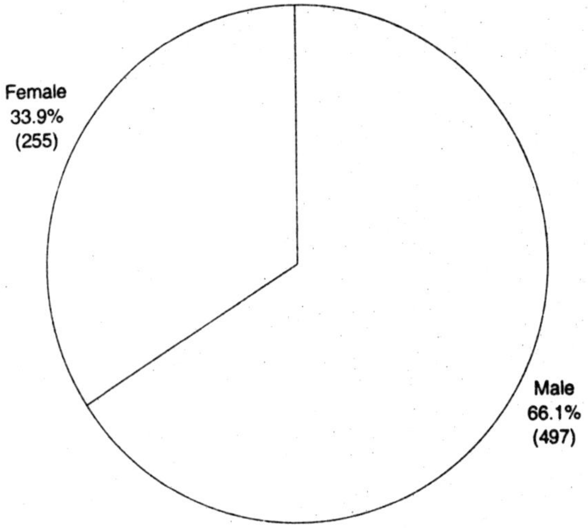

Total

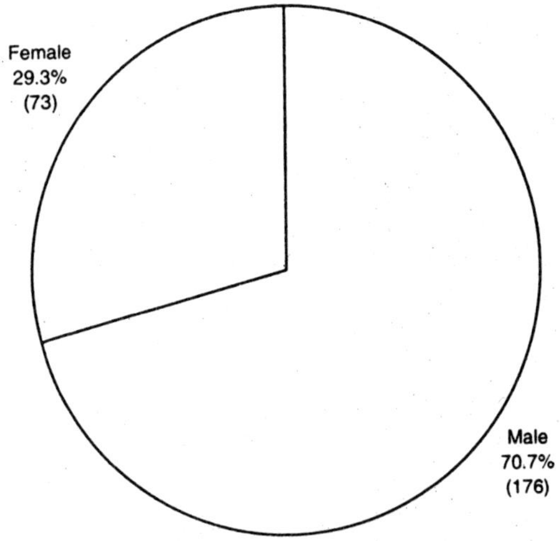

North Bihar

CHART 1 *(Contd.)*

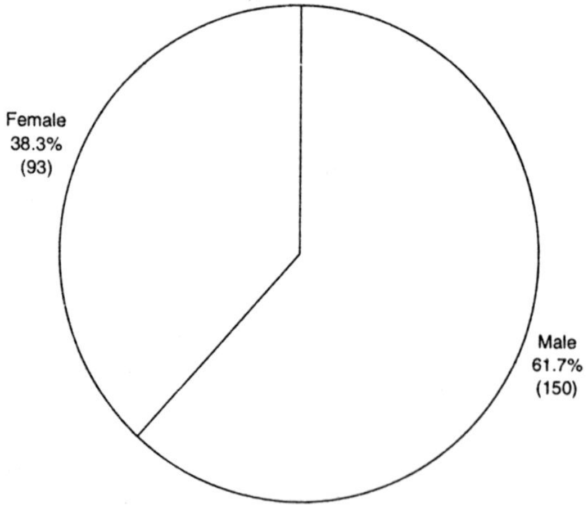

Central Bihar

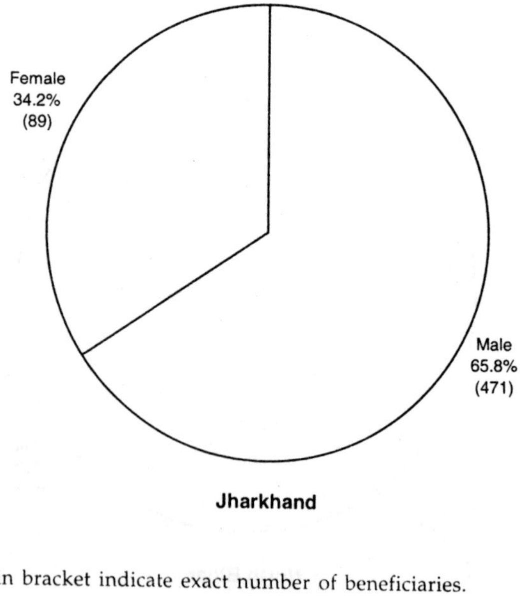

Jharkhand

NB : Figures in bracket indicate exact number of beneficiaries.

CHART 2

Categorisation of Beneficiaries of Poverty Alleviation Progarmmes

Literacy

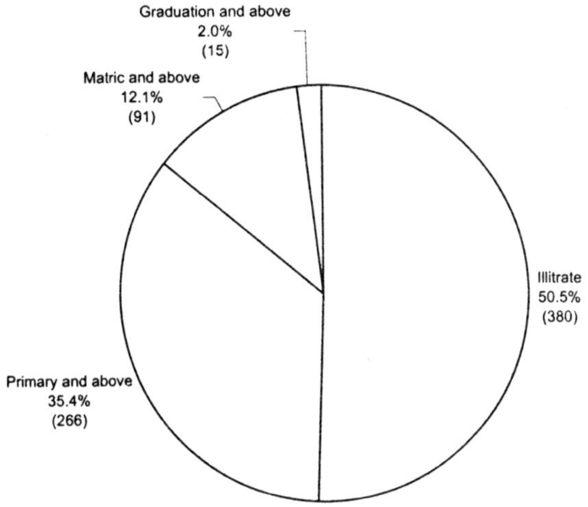

Total

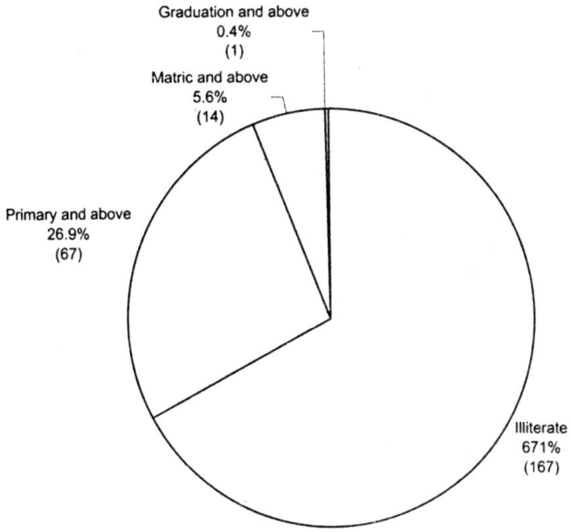

North Bihar

CHART 2 *(Contd.)*

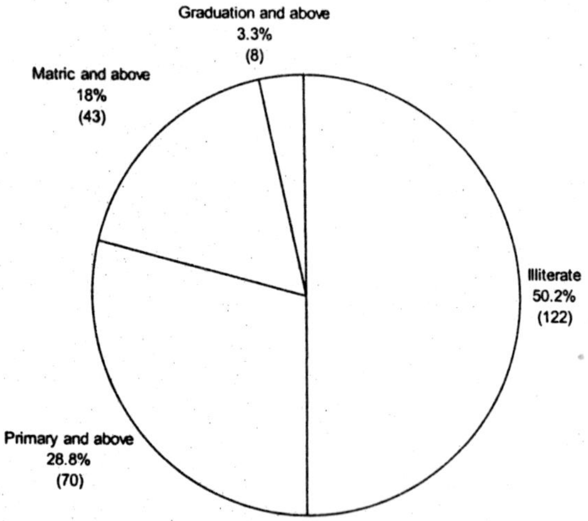

Central Bihar

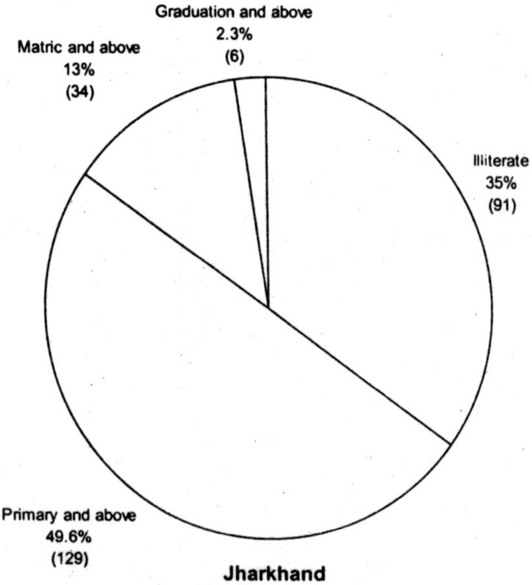

Jharkhand

NB : Figures in bracket indicate exact number of beneficiaries.

CHART 3

Categorisation of Beneficiaries of Poverty Alleviation Progarmmes

Occupation

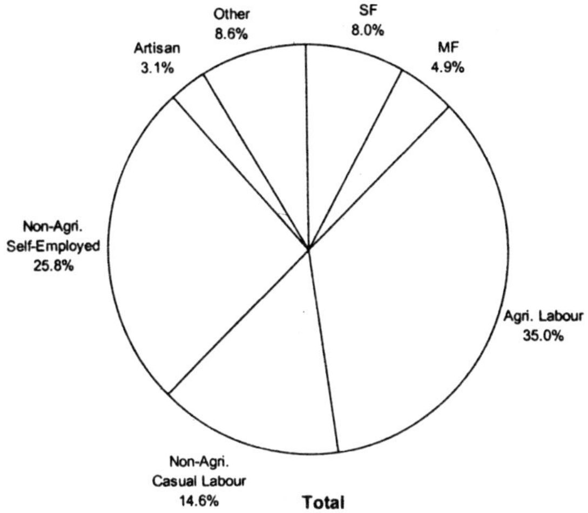

Total

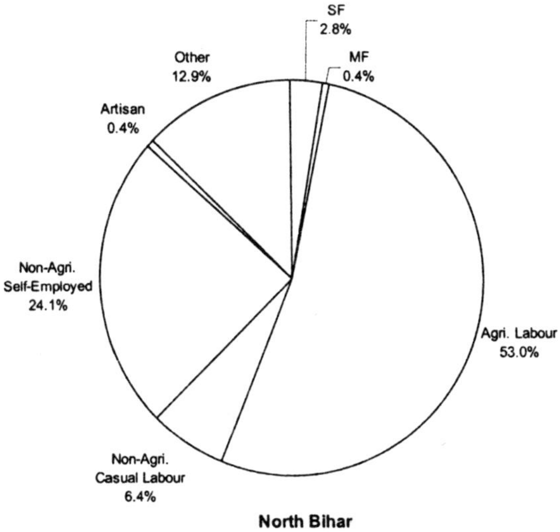

North Bihar

CHART 3 (*Contd.*)

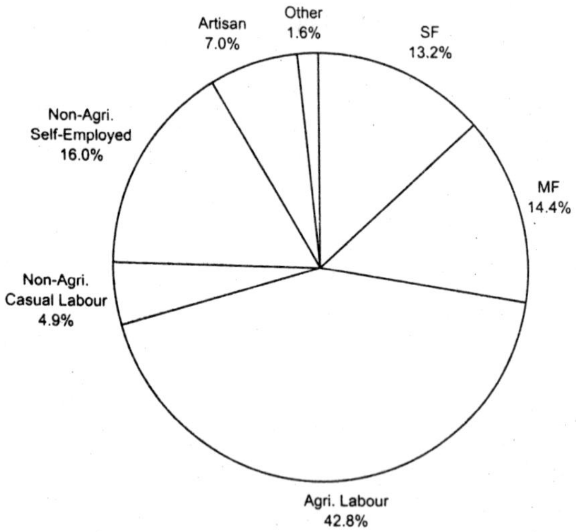

Central Bihar

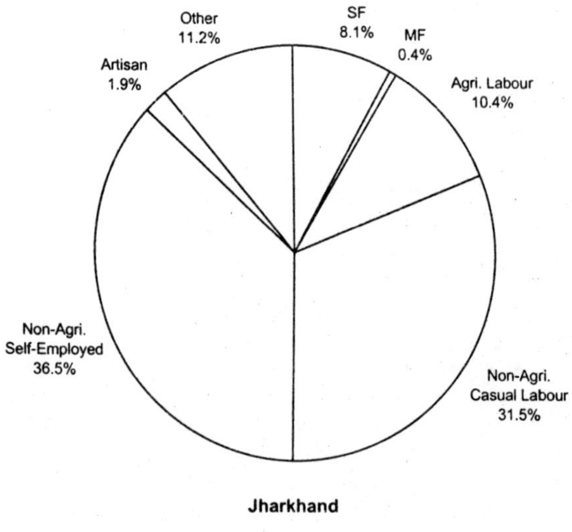

Jharkhand

NB : Figures in bracket indicate exact number of beneficiaries.

CHART 4

Categorisation of Beneficiaries of Poverty Alleviation Progarmmes

Size of Family

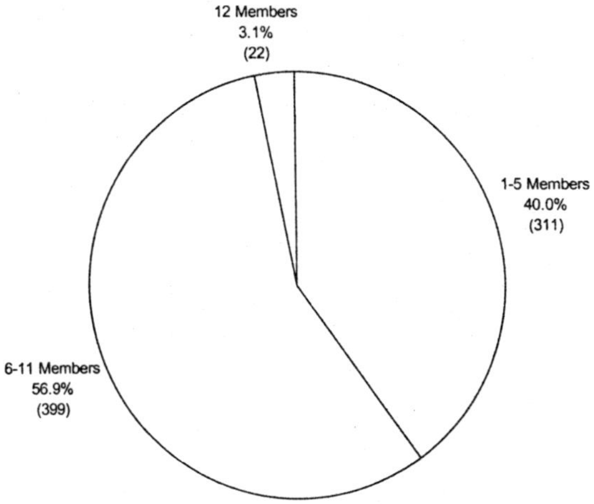

Total

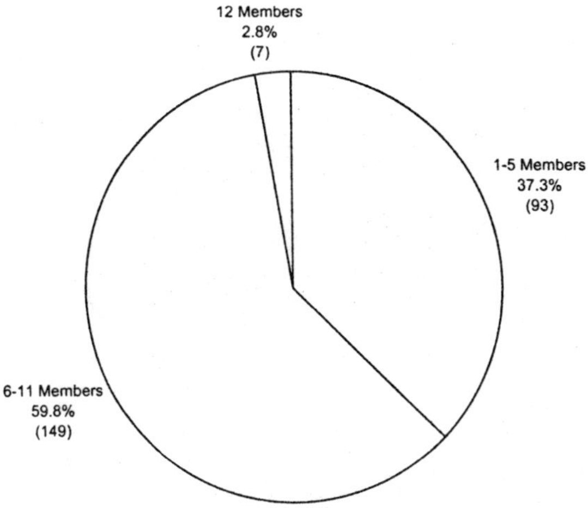

North Bihar

CHART 4 *(Contd.)*

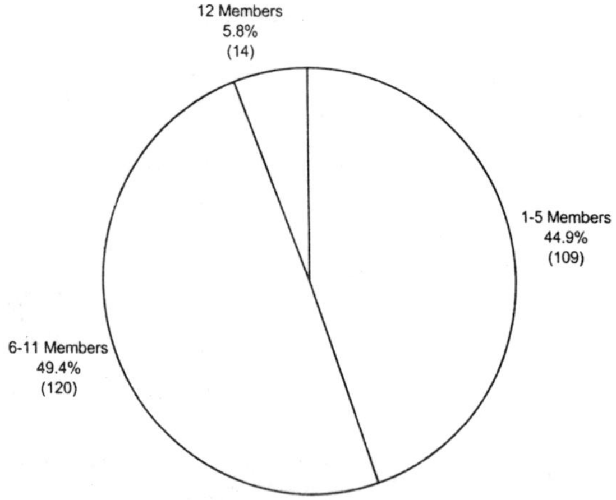

Central Bihar

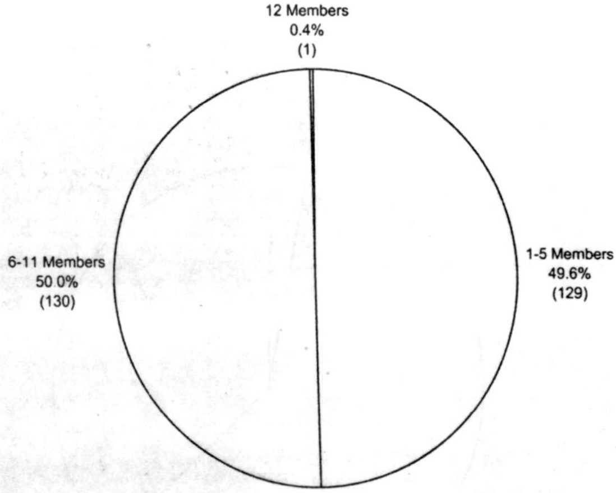

Jharkhand

NB : Figures in bracket indicate exact number of beneficiaries.

CHART 5

Social Classification of Beneficiaries

Category I

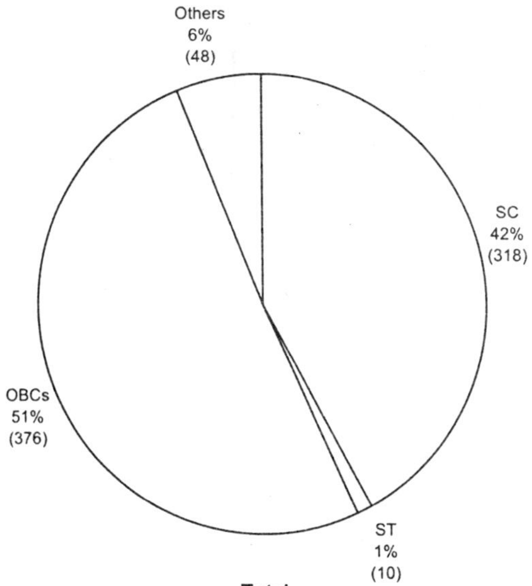

Total

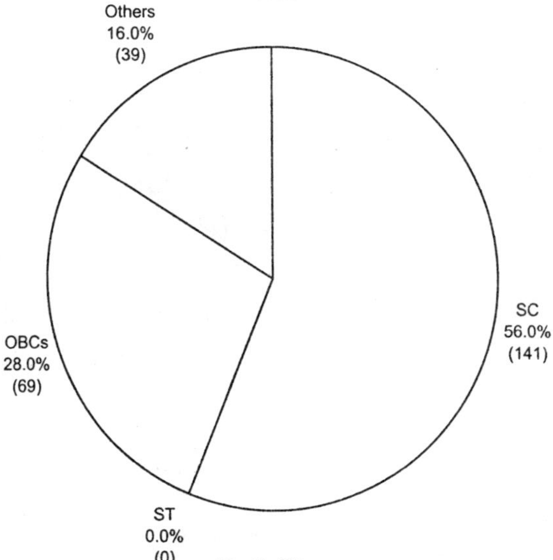

North Bihar

CHART 5 *(Contd.)*

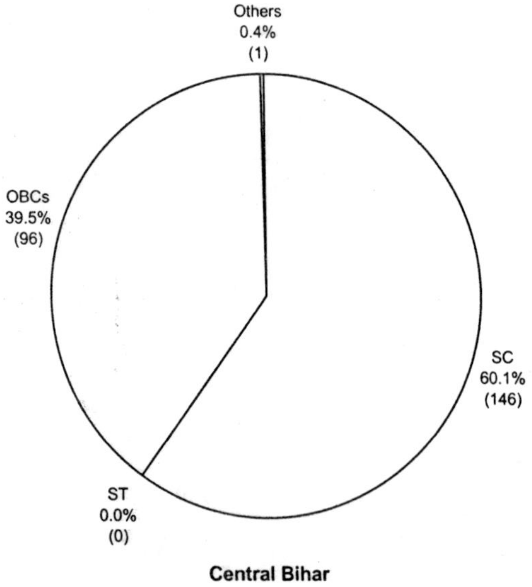

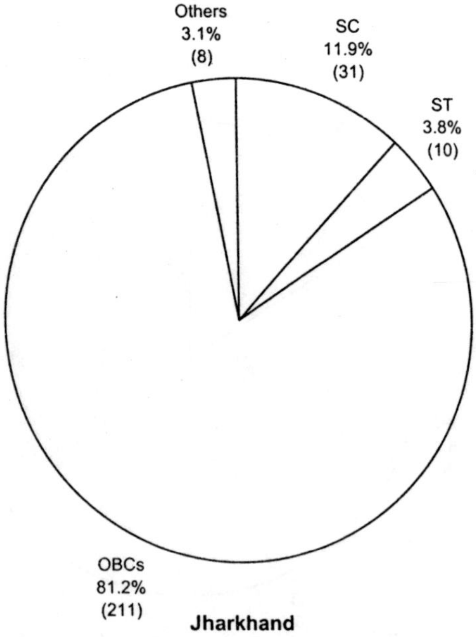

NB : Figures in bracket indicate exact number of beneficiaries.

CHART 6

Social Classification of Beneficiaries

Category II

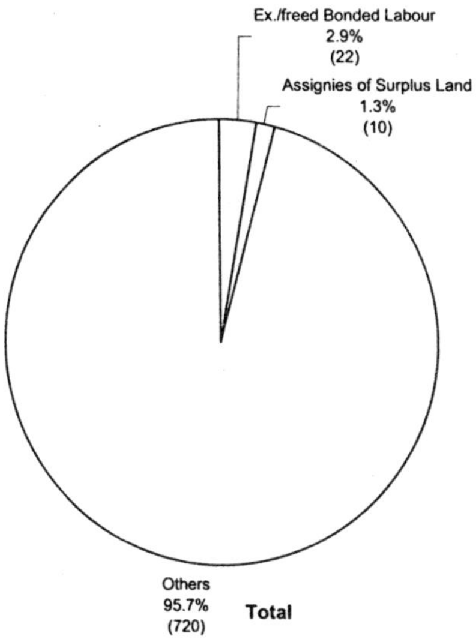

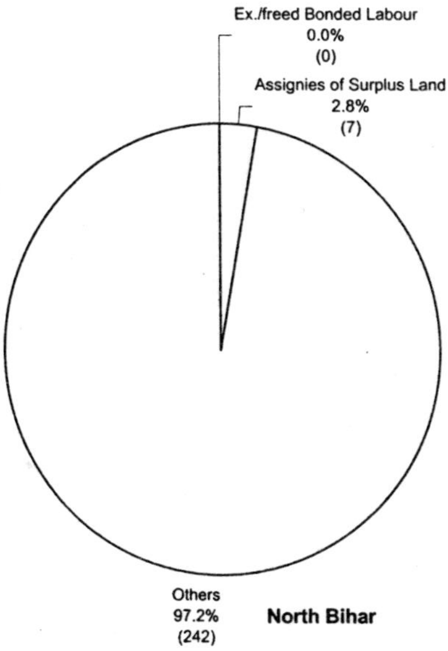

CHART 6 *(Contd.)*

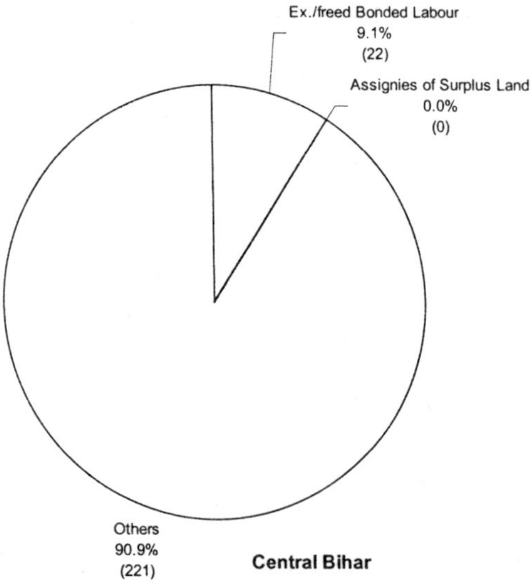

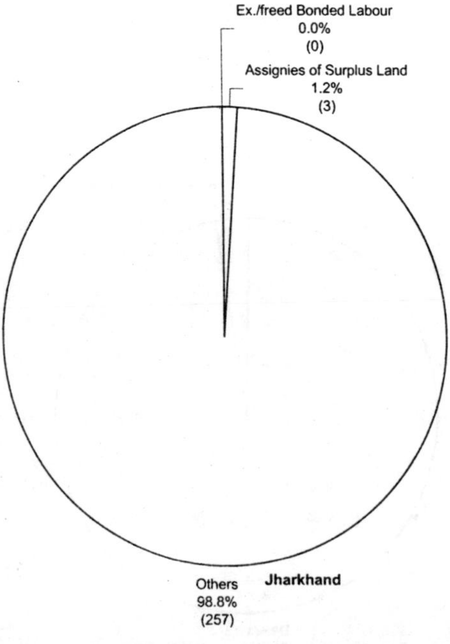

NB : Figures in bracket indicate exact number of beneficiaries.

CHART 7

Actual Family Income of Beneficiary

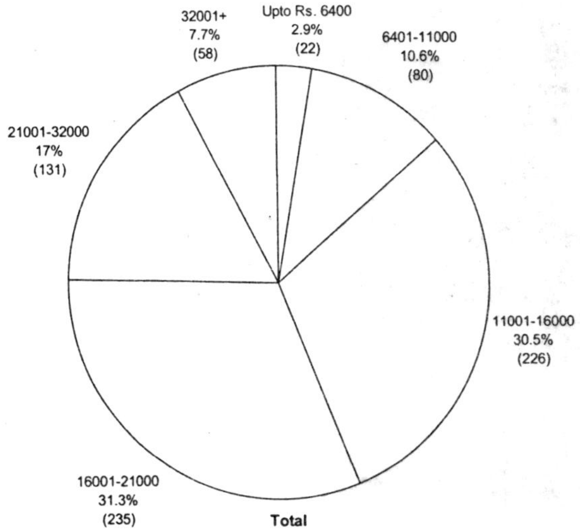

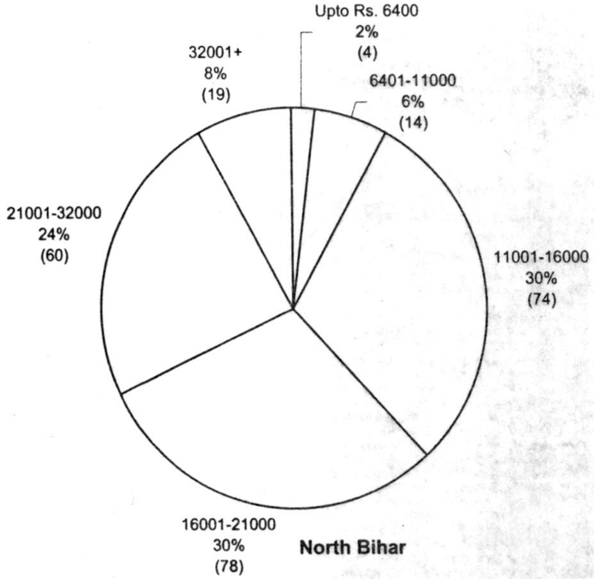

CHART 7 (Contd.)

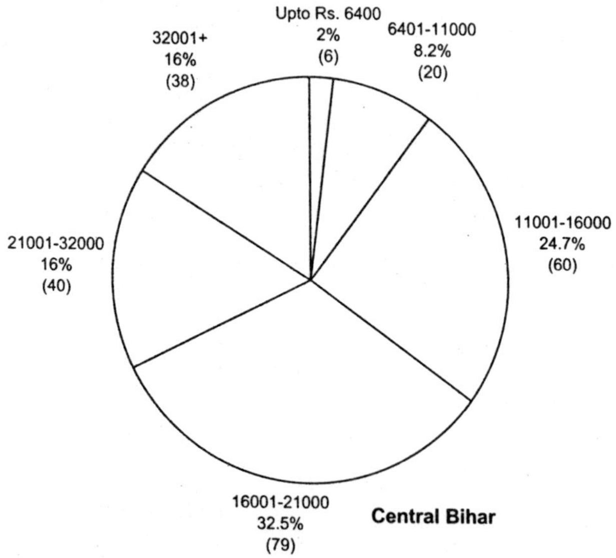

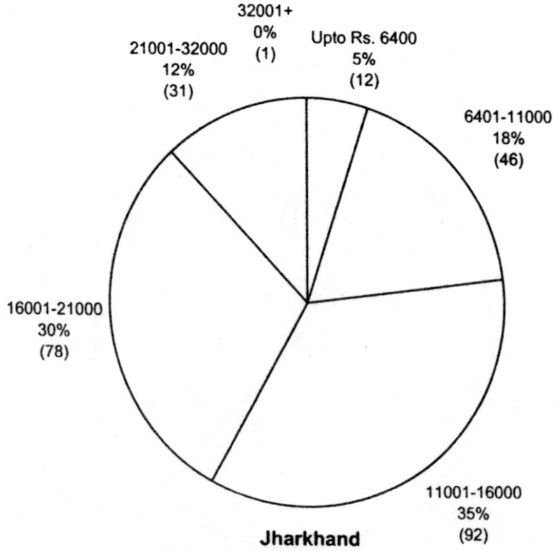

using the suitable deflators. During the Seventh Five Year Plan the Poverty line was fixed at Rs. 6400 per annum (for the family of 5 members). The amount was deflated to Rs. 11000 per annum at 1991-92 prices. The planning commission has adopted a new methodology using a state-specific price index for estimation of poverty line since 1993. Using this methodology the poverty line was at Rs. 16000 per annum at 1996-97 prices and Rs. 21000 per annum at 2000 prices for Bihar.

Only 22 (2.93%) beneficiaries had income below Rs. 6401, 80 (10.63%) beneficiaries had income in between Rs. 6401-11000, 226 (30.45%) beneficiaries had income in between Rs. 11001-16000 and 235 (31.21%) had income in between Rs. 16001-21000. Remaining 189 (25.13%) beneficiaries had income above poverty line. But they had managed to take the help from the poverty alleviation Programmes with their fraudulent skill. (Chart 7)

But it is a fact that a large number of households in rural areas have not been covered under poverty alleviation Programmes as they don't fall in the BPL category by living just above the poverty line. The Government has launched credit-cum - subsidy scheme covering people upto twice the income level of the BPL families. The scheme was launched with effect from April, 1999 with rural family annual income-ceiling upto Rs. 32000. Out of the beneficiaries having income above poverty line, 131 (17.42%) came to this category but 58 (7.71%) beneficiaries had income even beyond this.

Calculation of Poverty Indices of beneficiaries: *

Head-Count ratio :

$$H = \frac{q}{n} = \frac{570}{752} = 0.76$$

Income-gap ratio :

$$I = \frac{g}{\pi . q} = \frac{4132500}{21000 \times 570} = \frac{413.25}{1197}$$

$$I = 0.34$$

* (See technical notes for details).

Ginni Co-efficient :

$$G = 0.19$$

The Sen Index (P)

$$P = H \{I + (1-I) G\}$$

$$= 0.76 [0.34 + (1-0.34) 0.19]$$

$$= 0.76 [0.34 + 0.66 \times 0.19]$$

$$= 0.76 [0.34 + 0.12]$$

$$= 0.76 \times 0.46$$

$$= 0.35$$

An Analysis of Poverty Index

The calculation of Head-Count Ratio (H) for the state as a whole under different poverty alleviation Programmes shows that 76% of the beneficiaries were below poverty line. The estimated value of Income gap ratio (I) comes out ot be 0.34 which signifies that a large proportion of beneficiaries were in the upper income slab below poverty line.

A low estimate of Ginni coefficient (G) of 0.19 reflects a very low degree of income disparity among the beneficiaries below poverty line.

The Sen-Index being calculated on the basis of above information gives a value of 0.35 which also reveals that a considerable number of beneficiaries comes from the upper income slab below poverty line.

Socio-economic condition of North Bihar

249 beneficiaries were surveyed at the North Bihar unit. 176 (70.68%) beneficiaries were male and 73 (29.31%) were female. 82 (32.93%) beneficiaries were literate and 167 (67.06%) were illiterate. Out of 82 literate population 67 (81.70%) had only primary education i.e., below matriculation and 14 (17.07%) had secondary and senior secondary education and 1 (1.21%) had graduation degree. 7 (8.53%) beneficiaries were small farmers, 1 (0.04%) was marginal farmer, 132 (53.01%) were agricultural labourers. 16 (6.42%) were non-agricultural casual labourers, 60 (24.07%) were non-agricultural self

FIG. 1.1

Income Inequality for the Beneficiaries of Different Poverty Alleviation Programmes

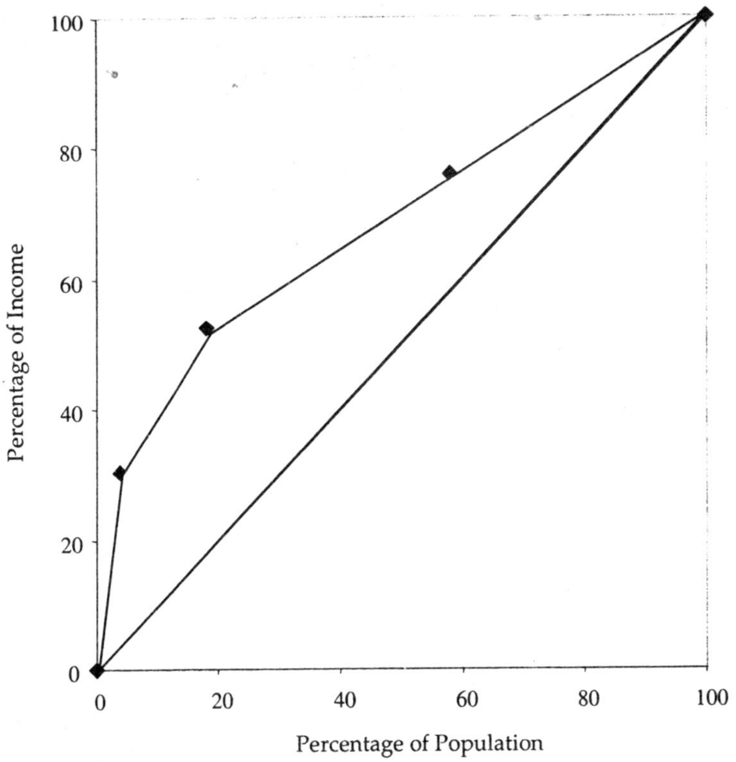

Percentage of Population	Percentage of Income
0	0
3.9	30.48
18.18	52.38
58.26	76.19
100	100

employed, 1 (0.40%) was artisan and 32 (12.85%) were others including mainly housewives. (Charts 1-3)

93 (37.34%) beneficiaries had a family size of 1-5 members, 149 (59.83%) had family size of 6-11 members and only 07 (2.81%) had a family size of 12 or more. 141 (56.62%) beneficiaries were scheduled caste, 69 (27.71%) were OBCs and 39 (15.66%) belonged to others including minorities. only 7 (2.81%) beneficiaries were assignees of surplus land and remaining 24 (97.18%) were of others/general categories. (Charts 4-6)

Only 4 (1.60%) beneficiaries of North Bihar had income below Rs. 6401- 14 (5.62%) in between Rs. 6401-11000, 4 (1.60%) in between Rs. 11001-16000 and 78 (31.32%) in between Rs. 16001-21000, 79 (31.72%) beneficiaries had income above poverty line but 60 (75.94%) had income in between Rs. 21001-32000 whereas 19 (24.05%) above Rs. 32001. (Chart 7)

Calculation of Poverty Indices : (North Bihar)

Head-Count ratio :

$$H = \frac{q}{n} = \frac{174}{248} = 0.70$$

Income-gap ratio :

$$I = \frac{g}{\pi . q} = \frac{1226600}{21000 \times 174} = \frac{1226.6}{3654}$$

$I = 0.33$

Ginni Coefficient :

$G = 0.22$

Sen-Index :

$$\begin{aligned} P &= H \{I + (1\text{-}I)\ G\} \\ &= 0.70\ [0.33 + (1\text{-}0.33) \times 0.22] \\ &= 0.70\ [0.33 + 0.67 \times 0.22] \\ &= 0.70\ [0.33 + 0.15] \\ &= 0.70 \times 0.48 \\ &= 0.33 \end{aligned}$$

FIG. 1.2

Income Inequality of Beneficiaries of Poverty Alleviation Programme in North Bihar

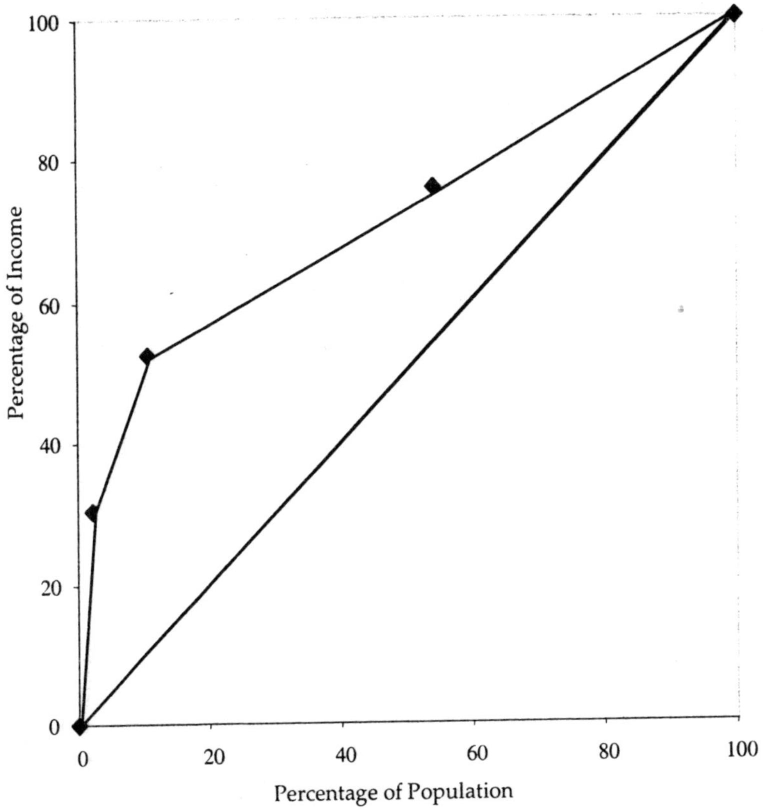

Percentage of Population	Percentage of Income
0	0
2.35	30.48
10.59	52.38
54.18	76.19
100	100

An Analysis of Poverty Index for North Bihar

The estimated value of Head-Count ratio (H) reflects that 70% of the beneficiaries were below poverty line. A value of 0.33 for Income gap ratio (I) reveals that a considerable number of beneficiaries were in the upper income slab below poverty line.

The Ginni coefficient (G) value is 0.22. This shows a very low degree of income inequality among the beneficiaries below poverty line.

The Sen-Index value of 0.33 also symbolizes that a large number of beneficiaries were in the upper income slab below poverty line.

Socio-economic Condition of Central Bihar

243 beneficiaries had been surveyd at the Central Bihar unit. Out of 243 beneficiaries, 150 (61.72%) beneficiaries were male and 93 (38.27%) were female. 121 (49.79%) were literate and 122 (50.20%) were illiterate. Out of 121 literate population, 70 (50.20%) had only primary education i.e., below matriculation level and 43 (35.53%) had the secondary and senior secondary education and 08 (6.61%) had graduation degree. Out of 243 beneficiaries, 32 (13.16%) were small farmers, 35 (14.40%) were marginal farmers, 104 (42.79%) were agricultural labourers, only 12 (4.93%) were non-agricultural casual labourers, 39 (16.04%) were non-agricultural self-employed, 17 (6.99%) were artisans and remaining only 4 (1.64%) were others including housewives. (Charts 1-3)

109 (44.85%) beneficiaries had the family size of 1-5 members, 120 (49.38%) had the family size of 6-11 members and only 14 (5.76%) had a family size of 12 or more. 146 (60.08%) beneficiaries were scheduled caste, 96 (39.50%) were OBCs, and only 1 (0.41%) belonged to others including minorities. Only 22 (9.05%) beneficiaries were ex/freed bonded labourers and remaining 221 (90.04%) were of others/ general categories. (Charts 4-6)

Only 6 (2.46%) beneficiaries of Central Bihar had income below Rs. 6401, 20 (8.23%) in between Rs. 6401-11000, 60 (24.69%) in between Rs. 11001-16000 and 79 (32.51%) in between Rs. 16001-21000. 78 (32.09%) beneficiaries had income above poverty line but 40 (16.46%) had income in between Rs. 21001-

32000 whereas 38 (15.63%) above Rs. 32001. (Chart 7)

Calculation of Poverty Indices : (Central Bihar)

Head-Count ratio :

$$H = \frac{q}{n} = \frac{168}{243} = 0.69$$

Income-gap ratio :

$$I = \frac{g}{\pi . q} = \frac{1108900}{21000 \times 168} = \frac{1108.9}{3528}$$

$I = 0.31$

Ginni Coefficients :

$G = 0.21$

Sen-Index :

$P = H \{I + (1\text{-}I)\ G\}$

$= 0.69\ [0.31 + (1\text{-}0.31) \times 0.21]$

$= 0.69\ [0.31 + 0.69 \times 0.21]$

$= 0.69\ [0.31 + 0.14]$

$= 0.69 \times 0.45$

$= 0.31$

An Analysis of Poverty Index for Central Bihar

The calculation of Head-Count ratio (H) shows that 69% of the beneficiaries were below poverty line. The estimated value of Income-gap ratio is 0.31. This value shows that a large number of beneficiaries were in the upper income slab below poverty line.

A value of 0.21 for Ginni co-efficient gives a low degree of income inequality among the beneficiaries below poverty line. The value of Sen-Index 0.31 signifies that a large number of beneficiaries were in the upper income group below poverty line. The equal values for Income-gap ratio and Sen index gives the same result numerically.

FIG. 1.3

Income Inequality of Beneficiaries of Poverty Alleviation Programme in Central Bihar

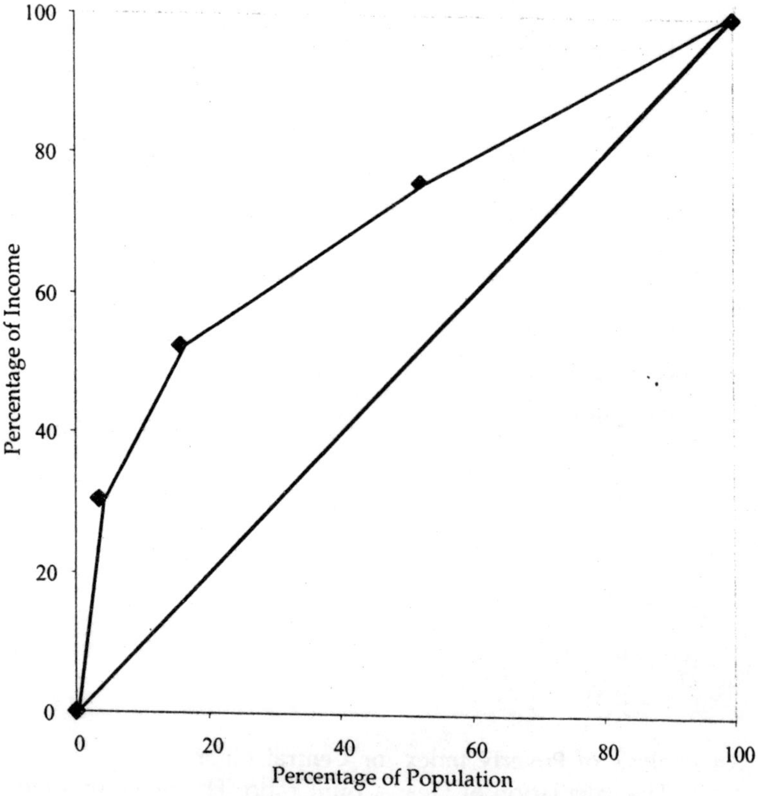

Percentage of Population	Percentage of Income
0	0
3.64	30.48
15.76	52.38
52.12	76.19
100	100

Socio-economic condition of Jharkhand

260 beneficiaries had been surveyed at Jharkhand unit. Out of 260 beneficiaries, 171 (65.76%) beneficiaries were male and 89 (34.23%) were female. 169 (65.0%) beneficiaries were literate and 91 (35.0%) were illiterate. Out of 169 beneficiaries 129 (76.33%) had the primary level education but below matriculation, 34 (20.11%) had the secondary and senior secondary level of education but below graduation and lastly, only 6 (3.55%) had the education of graduation level. Out of 260 beneficiaries 21 (08.07%) were small farmers, only a single (00.38%) was marginal farmer, 27 (10.38%) were agricultural labourers, 82 (31.53%) were non-agricultural casual labourers, 95 (36.53%) were non-agricultural self employed and only 5 (1.92%) were artisans and remaining 29 (11.15%) were others including housewives. (Chart 1-3)

Out of 260 beneficiaries , 129 (49.61%) had the family size of 1-5 members, 130 (50.0%) had the family size of 6-11 members, and only a single (00.38%) had the size of 12 or more. 31 (11.92%) beneficiaries were scheduled caste, 10 (3.84%) were scheduled tribes, 211 (1.15%) belonged to OBCs and only 8 (3.07%) were others including minorities. Only 3 (1.15%) were he assignies of surplus land and remaining 257 (98.84%) were of others/general category. (Chart 4-6)

12 (4.61%) beneficiaries of Central Bihar had income below Rs. 6401, 46 (17.69%) had in between Rs. 6401-11000, 92 (35.38%) had in between Rs. 11001-16000, 78 (30.0%) had in between Rs. 16001-21000. 32 (12.30%) beneficiaries had income above poverty line but 31 (11.92%) had income in between Rs. 21001-32000, and only 1 (0.38%) had above Rs. 32001. (Chart 7)

Calculation of Poverty Indices : (Jharkhand)

Head-Count ratio :

$$H = \frac{q}{n} = \frac{228}{260} = 0.87$$

Income-gap ratio :

$$I = \frac{g}{\pi . q} = \frac{1787000}{21000 \times 228} = \frac{1787}{4788}$$

I = 0.37

Ginni Co-efficients :

G = 0.15

Sen-Index :

$$P = H \{I + (1-I) G\}$$

$$= 0.87 [0.37 + (1-0.37) \times 0.15]$$

$$= 0.87 [0.37 + 0.63 \times 0.15]$$

$$= 0.87 [0.37 + 0.09]$$

$$= 0.87 \times 0.46$$

$$= 0.40$$

An Analysis of Poverty Index for Jharkhand

The calculation of Head-Count Ratio (H) for the Jharkhand region shows that 87% of the beneficiaries were below poverty line. The calculation of Income-gap ratio (I) gives a value of 0.37. The estimate reveals that a sufficiently large number of beneficiaries were in the higher income group below poverty line.

The measurement of Ginni co-efficients - 0.15, signifies a very low degree of income disparity among the beneficiaries below poverty line. The Sen-Index gives a value of 0.40 which also says that a large proportion of beneficiaries come from the upper income slab below poverty line.

However, the figure for Sen-Index gives a better picture as compared to Income-gap ratio.

FIG. 1.4

Income Inequality of Beneficiaries of Poverty Alleviation Programme in Jharkhand

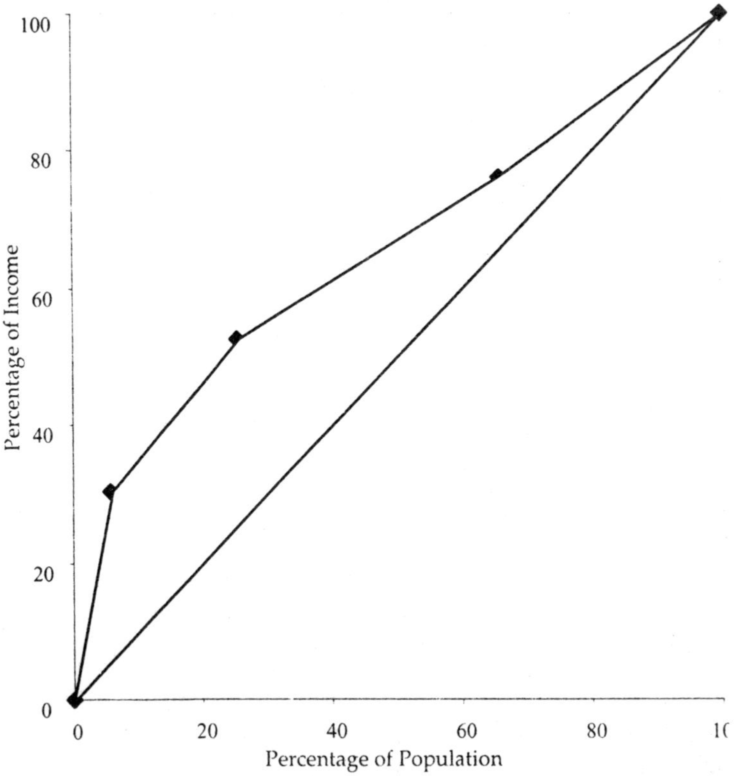

Percentage of Population	Percentage of Income
0	0
5.26	30.48
25.44	52.38
65.79	76.19
100	100

CHAPTER

2

SELF EMPLOYMENT PROGRAMMES

A. SWARNAJAYANTI GRAM SWAROZGAR YOJANA (SGSY)/ INTEGRATED RURAL DEVELOPMENT PROGRAMME (IRDP)

The Integrated Rural Development Programme (IRDP) was aimed at providing self-employment to the rural poor through acquisition of productive assets or appropriate skills which would generate additional income on a sustained basis to enable them cross the poverty line. Assistance was provided in the form of subsidy and bank credit. The target group consisted largely of small and marginal farmers, agricultural labourers and rural artisans living below the poverty line. Within the target group, there was an assured coverage of 50 percent for scheduled castes/scheduled tribes, 40 percent for women and 3 percent for the physically handicapped. Priority in assistance was also given to the families belonging to the assignees of ceiling surplus land, Green card holders covered under the Family Welfare Programme and freed bonded labourers.

IRDP was a centrally sponsored scheme which had been in operation in all the blocks of the country since 1980. Under the scheme central funds were allocated to states on the basis of ratio of rural poor in a state to the total poor in the country.

Under the Ninth Plan Programme it was decided to convert IRDP into a holistic programme covering all aspects of self-employment, namely, organisation of beneficiaries and their capacity building, planning of activity clusters, infrastructure, technology, credit and marketing by merger of existing sub-schemes—Training of Rural Youth for Self-Employment (TRYSEM), Development of Women and Children in Rural Areas (DWCRA), Supply of Improved Toolkits to Rural Artisans (SITRA) and Ganga Kalyan Yojana (GKY) into IRDP. It was also decided to shift from an individual beneficiary approach to a group and cluster approach.

Keeping in view the Ninth Plan Programme a Swarnajayanti Gram Swarozgar Yojana (SGSY) was launched with effect from April 1999 with the merger of IRDP, TRYSEM, DWCRA, GKY, SITRA, MWS (Million Wells Scheme) into it with the following objectives :

(i) focussed approach to poverty alleviation,
(ii) capitalising advantages of group lending; and
(iii) overcoming the problems associated with multiplicity of programmes.

The SGSY is conceived as a holistic programme of micro enterprises covering all aspects of self-employment which includes organising rural poor into Self-Help Groups (SHGs). It integrates various agencies like—District Rural Development Agencies, banks, line departments, Panchayati Raj Institutions (PRIs), non-governmental organisations, and other semi-government organisations. The objective of SGSY is to bring the existing poor families above the poverty line by providing them income generating assets through a mix of bank credit and government subsidy and to ensure that an assisted family has a month net income of at least Rs. 2000. Subsidy under SGSY is uniform at 30 percent of the project cost subject to a maximum of Rs 7500/- .In respect of SCs/STs, it is 50 percent subject to a maximum of Rs 10,000. For groups, the subsidy of 50 percent subject to a ceiling of Rs 1.25 lakh. There is no monetary limit on subsidy for irrigation projects. SGSY is funded by the centre and states in the ratio of 75:25.

In this background IRDP, which had been in existence since 1980, has been merged into SGSY with effect from April, 1999. The study has evaluated the performance of IRDP - the main scheme for self-employment with an objective to suggest viable measures for successful implementation of SGSY. Analysis of the data has been made under the following four sections :

(a) Socio-economic condition of the beneficiaries.
(b) Economic structure and viability of the scheme.
(c) General observations and recommendations.
(d) Calculation of poverty indices and its analysis.

(a) Socio-economic Condition of Beneficiaries

Institutional factors had dominant role in the process of development. Out of 180 beneficiaries, 161 (89.4%) were male and 19 (10.6%) were female. The least participation of women was prevalent in all the three sample zones, i.e., North Bihar, Central Bihar, and Jharkhand.

61.1% beneficiaries were literate while 38.9% were illiterate. Out of 61.1% literate population, 35.5% had education below matriculation level, 21.6% had qualification of matriculation and above but below graduation level. Only 3.9% had qualification of graduation and above. Illiteracy level was higher in North Bihar where 66.6% of the beneficiaries were illiterate. And out of the remaining 33.4% literate population 28.3% had only primary education, only 5.0% had matriculation and above qualification but below the graduation level.

Out of 180 beneficiaries 5.0% were small farmers, 11.2% were marginal farmers, 29.5% were agricultural labourers, 7.2% were non-agricultural casual labourers, 37.2% were non-agricultural self employed, 2.7% were artisans, and 7.2% were others. Agricultural labourers and non-agricultural self-employed had taken maximum benefit of the scheme. Marginal farmers had taken benefit of the scheme only in Central Bihar zone, where 18 persons (30.0% of the beneficiaries) of the zone were marginal farmers (Table 2A.1)

45.6% beneficiaries had the family size of 1-5 persons', 52.2% had the size of 6-11 persons and only 2.2 % had the size of 12 or more. Hence only 4 beneficiaries (2.2%) belonged to the combined family. The trend was almost similar in all the three sample zones.

70 (38.9%) beneficiaries belonged to scheduled castes and 100 (55.9%) belonged to OBCs. Only one (0.6%) beneficiary

TABLE 2A.1

Categorisation of Beneficiaries

Zone	Sex		Literacy		Literacy Level			Beneficiary's Occupation at the Time of Selection						
	Male	Female	Literate	Illiterate	Primary & above	Matric & above	Graduation & above	SF	MF	Agri-Labour	Non-agri. Casual Labour	Non-agri. Self employed	Artisan	Others
North Bihar	55	05	20	40	17	03	00	02	01	31	02	22	01	01
Central Bihar	51	09	42	18	21	16	05	06	18	14	05	12	04	01
Jharkhand	55	05	48	12	26	20	02	01	01	08	06	33	00	11
Total	161	19	110	70	64	39	07	09	20	53	13	67	05	13

belonged to scheduled tribes and 9 (5.0%) belonged to other caste groups including minorities. Hence OBCs had taken maximum benefit of the IRDP followed by scheduled caste group. Scheduled caste population was very small in the Jharkhand region. 50 (83.3%) of three total beneficiaries of the region belonged to OBCs category.

Priority under the scheme was to be given to the freed bonded labourers and assignees of surplus land. But only 4 beneficiaries (2.2%) were freed bonded labourers and only 2 (1.1%) were assignees of surplus land. Remaining 174 (96.7%) belong to other categories. (Table 2A.2)

Only 11 (6.11%) beneficiaries had income below Rs. 6401. 31 (17.22%) beneficiaries had income in between Rs. 6401/- to Rs. 11000/-. 56 (31.1%) beneficiaries had income in between Rs. 11001 to Rs. 16000. and 43 (23.88%) in between Rs. 16001 to Rs. 21000. 22 (12.22%) beneficiaries had income above Rs. 21000 but below Rs. 32000. 17 (9.4%) beneficiaries had income above Rs. 32000.Hence 39 beneficiaries had managed the IRDP loan by their skill, though they did not come under the purview of the scheme on the basis of their income. The most remarkable point was that not a single beneficiary from Jharkhand region had an income above Rs. 32000. In this region 6 (10.0%) beneficiaries had an income below Rs. 6401, 22 (36.6%) had an income in between Rs. 6401 to Rs. 11000, 24 (40.0%) in between Rs. 11001 to Rs. 16000 and 6 (10.0%) in between Rs. 16001 to Rs. 21000. Only 2 (3.3%) beneficiaries had an income in between Rs. 21001 to Rs. 32000/-. It seems that the better-off section had taken the benefit of the programme in sizeable proportion in North Bihar and Central Bihar zones. (Table 2 A.3)

Out of 180 beneficiaries, only 45 (25%) had non-institutional borrowing. Non-institutional borrowing was higher in Jharkhand region as 24 (53.3%) out of 45 beneficiaries who were in non-institutional debt belonged to that region. The main reasons for the non-institutional debt in the region are acquiring raw materials for the IRDP scheme and household consumption expenditure. Household consumption expenditure was the main reason for non-institutional debt in North Bihar and Central Bihar too. But the most significant aspect is that 135 (75.0%) beneficiaries had no outstanding non-institutional debt. (Table 2 A.4)

TABLE 2A.2

Size of the Family and Social Classification

Zone	*Size of the Family*			*Social Classification*						
				Category I				*Category II*		
	1-5	*6-11*	*12+*	*SC*	*ST*	*OBCs*	*Others*	*Ex/freed bonded labour*	*Assignies of surplus land*	*Others*
North Bihar	24	35	01	38	00	16	06	00	02	58
Central Bihar	24	34	02	26	00	34	00	04	00	56
Jharkhand	34	25	01	06	01	50	03	00	00	60
Total	82	94	04	70	01	100	09	04	02	174

TABLE 2A.3

Family Income

Zone	*Below Poverty Line*			*Above Poverty Line*		
	Upto 6400	*6401- 11000*	*11001- 16000*	*16001- 21000*	*21001- 32000*	*32001+*
North Bihar	03	02	20	23	09	03
Central Bihar	02	07	12	14	11	14
Jharkhand	06	22	24	06	02	00
Total	11	31	56	43	22	17

Out of 45 beneficiaries who were in non-institutional debt, 7 (15.5%) had debt in between Rs. 1000 to Rs. 2000, 25 (55.5%) in between Rs. 2001 to 5000, 11 (24.4%) in between Rs. 5001 to 10000. Only 1 (2.22%) in between Rs. 10001 to 15000 and the last 1 (2.22%) above Rs. 15001. 66% of the debtor beneficiaries of the Jharkhand region had outstanding debt in between Rs. 2001 to Rs. 5000. (Table 2A.5).

(b) Economic Structure and Viability of the Scheme

100% beneficiaries of IRDP had been selected through the V.L.W./ Block officials in North Bihar as well as in Jharkhand. But in Central Bihar only 16.6% i.e. 10 beneficiaries had been selected through the same. 58.3% (35) beneficiaries had been selected with the help of middlemen and remaining 25.0% i.e.15 beneficiaries through the Bank officials and others. Hence, middlemen had played a significant role in beneficiary selection in Central Bihar. Gram Sabha/Panchayati Raj Institutions played no role in the beneficiary selection in all the zones. (Table 2A.6).

100% beneficiaries had reported about Mandays wastage in connection with the scheme. 52.2% i.e.94 beneficiaries reported the Mandays wastage of 1-4 days, 33.3% i.e. 60 reported the wastage of 5-9 days, 11.66% i.e. 21 reported the wastage of 10-15 days and only 2.77% i.e. 5 reported the wastage of 16 or more days. The trend was almost similar in all the three zones. 35 (34 from Central Bihar and only 1 from North Bihar) beneficiaries reported that there was no Mandays

TABLE 2A.4

Beneficiary's Indebtedness

Zone	*Non-Institutional Borrowing*		*If Yes Reasons*						
	Yes	*No*	*Acquiring asset under the scheme*	*Acquiring raw material under the scheme*	*Maintenance of unit under the scheme*	*Repayment of Bank loan under the scheme*	*Household consumption*	*Repayment of pre - IRDP loan*	*Other needs*
North Bihar	06	54	00	00	00	00	04	00	02
Central Bihar	15	45	00	00	00	02	09	01	03
Jharkhand	24	36	01	15	00	00	08	00	00
Total	45	135	01	15	00	02	21	01	05

TABLE 2A.5

Beneficiary's Indebtedness

Zone	Amount of Outstanding Debt					
	Upto 1000	1001-2000	2001-5000	5001-10000	10001-15000	15001+
North Bihar	00	03	02	00	00	01
Central Bihar	00	02	07	05	01	00
Jharkhand	00	02	16	06	00	00
Total	00	07	25	11	01	01

TABLE 2A.6

Selection of Beneficiary

Zone	Selection of Beneficiary through					Whether Credit Camp was held for Completion of Loan Application Formalities	
	Gram Sabha/ Gram Panchayat	V.L.W./ Block officials	Bank officials	Middle Man	Others	Yes	No
North Bihar	00	60	00	00	00	00	60
Central Bihar	00	10	14	35	01	00	60
Jharkhand	00	60	00	00	00	00	60
Total	00	130	14	35	01	00	180

wastage at Block office level. The main reason was that these beneficiaries of Central Bihar had obtained IRDP help through the middlemen. 100% beneficiaries reported about Mandays wastage at the Bank level. 173 (96.1%) reported a Mandays wastage of 1-4 days at the Bank level. 4 (2.22%) reported a Mandays wastage of 5-9 days and 3 (1.66%) of 10-15 days. Only 8 (4.44%) reported Mandays wastage of 1 to 4 days at other offices. 109 (60.5%) beneficiaries reported Mandays wastage at market, out of which 101 (56.5%) reported Mandays wastage of 1-4 days at market. In monetary terms only 37 (20.5%) reported Mandays wastage upto Rs. 100. 80 (44.44%) in between

Rs. 101-200, 57 (31.66%) in between Rs. 201-500 and 6 (3.33%) above Rs. 500 (Table 2 A.7).

Only 5 (2.77%) beneficiaries reported that they did not incur any expenditure on visit to block, bank, other offices and market. 7 (3.88%) reported expenditure upto Rs. 25, 31 (17.22%) in between Rs. 26-50, 48 (26.66%) in between Rs. 51-100, 74 (41.1%) in between Rs. 101-500, 9 (5.0%) in between Rs. 501-1000 and 6 (3.33%) above Rs 1000. Only 20 (11.1%) beneficiaries paid no amount as a speed money in the process of getting IRDP assistance. 57 (31.66%) reported payment upto Rs. 500, 42 (23.33%) in between Rs. 501-1000, 31 (17.22%) in between Rs. 1001-2000, 19 (10.55%) in between Rs. 2001-3000, 10 (5.55%) in between Rs. 3001-5000 and only 1 (0.55) beneficiary of Central Bihar above Rs. 5000. Not even a single beneficiary of North Bihar and Jharkhand paid above Rs. 2000 as speed money (Table 2A.8).

89 (49.44%) beneficiaries had taken the scheme for primary sector under which 9 (5.0%) had taken for agriculture, 5 (2.77%) for irrigation, 66 (36.66%) for milch-animals, and 9 (5.05%) for animal husbandry excluding milch animals. 44 (73.3% beneficiaries of the zone) of Central Bihar and 19 (31.66% beneficiaries of the zone) of North Bihar had taken IRDP scheme for milch-animals whereas only 3 (5.0%) beneficiaries of Jharkhand had taken scheme for milch-animals. Only 18 (30.0%) beneficiaries had taken scheme for secondary sector, 10 (16.6%) for village industries and 8 (13.3%) for handicraft. The remaining 73 (40.55%) beneficiaries had taken IRDP scheme for tertiary sector. Out of which 19 (31.6%) beneficiaries of North Bihar and 41 (68.33%) of Jharkhand had taken IRDP schemes only for shops. In Jharkhand region the maximum beneficiaries had taken IRDP scheme for business purposes. In brief, 66 (36.66%) beneficiaries had taken IRDP scheme for milch-animals, 67 (37.22%) for shops and the remaining 47 (26.11%) beneficiaries had taken the scheme for different other activities. (Table 2A.9)

104 (57.77%) beneficiaries procured assets under the scheme, 46 (25.55%) did not procure any asset and in case of remaining 30 (16.6%) only working capital was required. 102 (56.66%) beneficiaries reported that the sanctioned amount of the scheme was adequate, 61 (33.88%) reported that the

TABLE 2A.7

Selection of Beneficiary

Zone	Mandays Wastage of Beneficiary																									Mandays wastage in terms of wage (Rs.)				
	Block office					Baank office					Other office					Market					Total									
	0	1-4	5-9	10-15	16+	0	1-4	5-9	10-15	16+	0	1-4	5-9	10-15	16+	0	1-4	5-9	10-15	16+	0	1-4	5-9	10-15	16+	0	1-100	101-200	201-500	501+
North Bihar	01	36	20	03	00	00	59	01	00	00	60	00	00	00	00	42	18	00	00	00	00	15	31	13	01	00	05	19	33	03
Central Bihar	34	16	05	05	00	00	54	03	03	00	59	01	00	00	00	21	31	07	01	00	00	34	14	08	04	00	22	17	18	03
Jharkhand	00	60	00	00	00	00	60	00	00	00	53	07	00	00	00	08	52	00	00	00	00	45	15	00	00	00	10	44	06	00
Total	35	112	25	08	00	00	173	04	03	00	172	08	00	00	00	71	101	07	01	00	00	94	60	21	05	00	37	80	57	06

TABLE 2A.8

Expenses to Mitigate the Loan

Zone	*Expenses by Beneficiary on Visit to Block office/Bank/other offices/markets*							*Payments of Speed Money*						
	0	*1-25*	*26-50*	*51-100*	*101-500*	*501-1000*	*1000+*	*0*	*1-500*	*501-1000*	*1001-2000*	*2001-3000*	*3001-5000*	*5001+*
North Bihar	00	00	01	19	35	05	00	08	26	23	03	00	00	00
Central Bihar	04	07	10	13	16	04	06	11	01	02	16	19	10	01
Jharkhand	01	00	20	16	23	00	00	01	30	17	12	00	00	00
Total	05	07	31	48	74	09	06	20	57	42	31	19	10	01

TABLE 2A.9

Sectoral Distribution of Assets

Zone	*Primary Sector*					*Secondary Sector*			*Tertiary Sector*			
	Agri-culture	*Irri-gation*	*Milch animal*	*Animal Husbandry excluding primary Milch animal*	*Total*	*Handi-craft*	*Village Industry*	*Total*	*Hotel*	*Shop*	*Tailoring*	*Total*
North Bihar	01	02	19	08	30	03	03	06	03	19	02	24
Central Bihar	06	01	44	00	51	00	02	02	00	07	00	07
Jharkhand	02	02	03	01	08	05	05	10	01	41	00	42
Total	09	05	66	09	89	08	10	18	04	67	02	73

sanctioned amount was inadequate and 17 (9.44%) reported that the sanctioned amount was inadequate due to extra expenditure including payment of speed money. (Table 2A.10)

131 (72.77%) beneficiaries reported that they had received assets under the scheme as per their choice. All the 60 (100%) beneficiaries of the Jharkhand reported this as they had received the sanctioned amount in cash. Only 8 (13.33%) beneficiaries of Central Bihar reported that they had not received assets as per their choice. All the 39 (65.0%) beneficiaries of North Bihar who procured assets had reported that assets had been supplied as per their choice. 38 (63.33%) beneficiaries of North Bihar had received good quality of assets and only 1 (1.66%) had received average quality of assets. In Central Bihar 16 (26/66%) received good quality of assets and 16 (26.66%) received average quality of assets whereas 8 (13.33%) received poor quality of assets including defective machines. The question did not arise in Jharkhand region since all had taken cash for the purchase of assets. 139 (77.2%) beneficiaries accepted that the assistance covered entire cost of the scheme, 41 (22.8%) reported that the assistance did not cover the entire cost of the scheme. 26 (63.41%) amongst them had managed the remaining amount from own sources whereas 15 (36.58%) managed the amount through borrowing. (Table 2A. 10a).

The loan amount was distributed by the Commercial Banks in all the three zones. All the beneficiaries of Central Bihar and Jharkhand had received loan pass book. But this was not distributed in North Bihar (Table 2A.11).

Mode of repayment for IRDP loan was monthly in case of 160 (88.88%) beneficiaries, quarterly in case of 6 (3.33%) beneficiaries, bi-annual in case of 4 (2.22%) beneficiaries and annual in case of 10 (5.55%) beneficiaries. 3 (1.66%) beneficiaries had to repay in 1-5 instalments, 10 (5.55%) beneficiaries in 6-10 instalments, 6 (3.33%) beneficiaries in 11-20 instalments, 48 (26.66%) beneficiaries in 21-36 instalments, and 113 (62.77%) beneficiaries in 37- 60 instalments. 62 (32.44%) beneficiaries had to repay within 36 months, 20 (11.1%) beneficiaries in 37- 48 months and 98 (54.44%) beneficiaries in between 49-60 months. Only 34 (18.88%) beneficiaries had repaid the instalments as per schedule and there was no overdues against them. Not even a

TABLE 2A.10

Procurement and Status of the Asset

Zone	*Asset*			*Cost of the Scheme*		
	Procured	*Not Procured*	*Not required due to only need of working capital*	*Adequate*	*Inadequate*	*Inadequate due to extra expenditure*
North Bihar	39	20	01	39	20	01
Central Bihar	40	18	02	38	06	16
Jharkhand	25	08	27	25	35	00
Total	104	46	30	102	61	17

single beneficiary in North Bihar came in this category whereas 21 (35%) beneficiaries of Central Bihar and 13 (21.66%) beneficiaries of Jharkhand came under the category. 30 (16.6%) beneficiaries had overdues in between 1-10 instalments, 35 (19.44%) in between 11-20 instalments, 26 (14.44%) in between 21-30 instalments, 18 (10.0%) in between 31-40 instalments and 37 (20.55%) in between 41-60 instalments. Not even a single beneficiary of Jharkhand had overdues in between 41- 60 instalments whereas 36 (60.0%) beneficiaries of North Bihar had overdues in between 41-60 instalments. Only 3 (5.0%) beneficiaries of Central Bihar had reported that the first payment schedule was before the gestation period. Remaining 177 (98.33%) beneficiaries had reported that the 1st payment schedule was after the gestation period (Table 2A.12).

Only 15 (8.33%) beneficiaries were satisfied with the terms and conditions of the loan, 101 (56.11%) were not aware of the terms and conditions and 64 (35.55%) were dissatisfied with the terms and conditions. Out of 64 dissatisfied beneficiaries 15 (23.43%) were dissatisfied due to high interest rate, 4 (6.25%) were due to time consuming procedure, 4 (6.25%) were dissatisfied due to inadequate amount and 41 (64.06%) were dissatisfied due to money demanded by the officials and the middlemen. (Table 2 A.12a)

TABLE 2A.10A

Procurement and Status of the Asset

Zone	Asset according to Beneficiary Choice			Quality of the Asset				Assistance Covered the Entire Cost of the Asset/Scheme		Source of Remaining Cost		
	Yes	No	N.A.	Good	Average	Poor	N.A.	Yes	No	Own Source	Borowing	N.A.
North Bihar	39	00	21	38	01	00	21	53	07	05	02	00
Central Bihar	32	08	20	16	16	08	20	51	09	05	04	00
Jharkhand	60	00	00	00	00	00	60	35	25	16	09	00
Total	131	08	41	54	17	08	101	139	41	26	15	00

TABLE 2A.11

Bank-wise Distribution of Loan

Zone	*Commercial Bank*	*Regional Rural Bank*	*Others*	*Total*	*Loan Pass book given to the Beneficiary*	
					Yes	*No*
North Bihar	60	00	00	60	00	60
Central Bihar	60	00	00	60	60	00
Jharkhand	60	00	00	60	60	00
Total	180	00	00	180	120	60

93 (51.66%) beneficiaries reported that the loan amount had been repaid by the income generated from the given assets under the scheme, 6 (3.33%) beneficiaries had repaid by disposal of old assets, 19 (10.55%) beneficiaries by old savings, 6 (3.33%) beneficiaries by borrowing from the relatives and friends, 17 (9.44%) beneficiaries by amount received from second dose of IRDP loan. 1 (0.55%) beneficiary had given no response, 38 (21.11%) respondents had not repaid any instalment. (Table 2A.12b).

4 (2.22%) beneficiaries had overdues upto Rs. 1000, 44 (24.44%) beneficiaries in between Rs. 1001-5000, 71 (39.44%) beneficiaries in between Rs. 5001-10000, 26 (14.44%) beneficiaries in between Rs. 10001-15000 and 1 (0.55%) beneficiary above Rs. 15000. There was no overdues against 34 (18.88%) beneficiaries. (Table 2A.13)

24 (13.33%) beneficiaries reported that they couldn't repay the loan as the assets were perished, 8 (4.44%) beneficiaries had emphasized on the delay in income-generation of the scheme as the main reason for overdues, 51 (28.33%) beneficiaries reported that inadequate income from the asset was the main reason of overdues, 3 (1.66%) beneficiaries had complained about lack of marketing facilities which caused overdues, 10 (5.55%) beneficiaries had mentioned the unforeseen calamity as the main reason of overdues, 3 (1.66%) beneficiaries could not repay the loan due to the burden of old dues. 47 (26.11%) beneficiaries could not explain the exact

TABLE 2A.12

Loan Repayment Schedule

Zone	*Mode of Repayment*				*Number of Installment*					*Repayment Period Month*				*Repayment of Installment*							*1st after gestation*	*Payment before gestation period*
															No. of instalment as overdues							
	Monthly	*Quarterly*	*Bi-annual*	*Annual*	*1-5*	*6-10*	*11-20*	*21-36*	*37-60*	*1-36*	*37-48*	*49-60*	*61+*	*As per schedule*	*0*	*1-10*	*11-20*	*21-30*	*31-40*	*41-60*		
North Bihar	50	00	00	10	03	07	00	00	50	07	18	35	00	00	00	10	06	05	03	36	00	60
Central Bihar	60	00	00	00	00	00	00	00	60	00	02	58	00	21	21	03	17	06	12	01	03	57
Jharkhand	50	06	04	00	00	03	06	48	03	55	00	05	00	13	13	17	12	15	03	00	00	60
Total	160	06	04	10	03	10	06	48	113	62	20	98	00	34	34	30	35	26	18	37	03	177

TABLE 2A.12A

Loan Repayment Schedule

Zone	*Beneficiary Satisfaction*		*Causes of Dissatisfaction*					
	Yes	*No*	*Not Aware*	*High interest rate*	*Time consuming procedure*	*Inadequate loan amount*	*Capacity for repayment not taken into account*	*Money demanded by officials/ middle men*
North Bihar	06	14	40	08	00	00	00	06
Central Bihar	07	19	34	07	00	01	00	11
Jharkhand	02	31	27	00	04	03	00	24
Total	15	64	101	15	04	04	00	41

TABLE 2A.12B

Loan Repayment Schedule

Zone	*How was the Loan Repaid*							
	Income generated from given assets	*Disposal of old assets*	*Old saving*	*Borrowing from friends/ relations*	*Borrowing from money lenders, traders, land lords*	*No response*	*Second dose of IRDP loan*	*Not repaid any instalment*
North Bihar	29	01	07	00	00	00	00	23
Central Bihar	21	05	07	04	00	01	17	05
Jharkhand	43	00	05	02	00	00	00	10
Total	93	06	19	06	00	01	17	38

TABLE 2A.13

Overdues

Zone	*Beneficiaries not in over dues*	*1-1000*	*1001-5000*	*5001-10000*	*10001-15000*	*15001+*
North Bihar	00	00	08	37	14	01
Central Bihar	21	01	12	16	10	00
Jharkhand	13	03	24	18	02	00
Total	34	04	44	71	26	01

reason of overdues. It seems that they were not serious about the repayment. (Table 2A.14).

Assets of only 77 (42.77%) beneficiaries were intact whereas assets of 103 (57.22%) beneficiaries were not intact. Out of 103 beneficiaries whose assets were not intact, 62 (34.44%) had not purchased the assets, 11 (6.11%) had sold the assets. Assets of 24 (13.33%) beneficiaries were fully perished. Assets of 1 (0.55%) beneficiary was defective and 5 (2.77%) beneficiaries had given different reasons. (Table 2A.15).

Reasons for not intact were personal and natural calamites in case of 6 beneficiaries, inadequate income was generated in case of 13 beneficiaries, high maintenance cost in case of 1 beneficiary, defective assets in case 5 beneficiaries, compulsive immediate household consumption requirement in case of 11 beneficiaries and others in case of 5 beneficiaries and lastly 62 beneficiaries did not purchase the assets. (Table 2A.15a) 151 beneficiaries were not aware about the insurance for IRDP but 29 beneficiaries had awareness about the said scheme. Assets of not a single beneficiary of North Bihar and Jharkhand were ensured, but the assets of 50% beneficiaries of Central Bihar were ensured. (Table 2A.16)

Only 9 (5.0%) beneficiaries had received any training to develop their skill. 125 (69.4%) beneficiaries had not received any training. And training was not required for 46 (25.5%) beneficiaries. Out of 9 trained beneficiaries, only 1 (11.11%) beneficiary of Jharkhand had received training under TRYSEM and 8 had received informal training. 8 beneficiaries had termed

TABLE 2A.14

Reasons for Overdues

Zone	Asset perished	Delay in Income generation from the scheme	Inadequate income for regular payment	Lack of marketing facilities	Unforeseen calamity	Old dues	Tight repayment schedule	Others/ Not explained
North Bihar	13	07	15	00	01	01	00	23
Central Bihar	06	00	13	00	06	01	00	13
Jharkhand	05	01	23	03	03	01	00	11
Total	24	08	51	03	10	03	00	47

TABLE 2A.15

Current Status of Assets

Zone	*Intact*	*No intact*	*If not intact current status*					
			Not purchased	*Sold*	*Fully perished*	*Defective*	*Transferred without sale*	*Others*
North Bihar	25	35	20	01	12	01	00	01
Central Bihar	30	30	18	06	06	00	00	00
Jharkhand	22	38	24	04	06	00	00	04
Total	77	103	62	11	24	01	00	05

Table 2A.15A

Reasons for not Intact

Zone	*Unexpected contigency/ personal natural calamities*	*Not enough Income was generated*	*Maintenance was costly*	*Defective*	*Cost of Maintenance was higher because Rise of Price of input required for Maintenance*	*Cost of Maintenance as anticipated, but it could not be afforded due to compulsive immediate house hold consumption requirement*	*Others*	*Not purchased*
North Bihar	00	11	01	01	00	00	02	20
Central Bihar	04	01	00	04	00	00	03	18
Jharkhand	02	01	00	00	00	11	00	24
Total	06	13	01	05	00	11	05	62

TABLE 2A.16

Insurance

Zone	Beneficiary awareness about the insurance for IRDP		Asset of Beneficiary	
	Yes	No	Insured	Not insured
North Bihar	00	60	00	60
Central Bihar	23	37	30	30
Jharkhand	06	54	00	60
Total	29	151	30	150

the training useful whereas 1 beneficiary had reported that the training was not useful (Table 2A.17).

137 (76.11%) beneficiaries had reported that the availability of input was adequate but 43 (23.88%) had complained about inadequacy of input supply in their areas. 148 (82.22%) beneficiaries had expressed that the marketing of output of the services was adequate. but 32 (17.77%) beneficiaries had expressed about inadequacy of marketing facilities. 103 (57.22%) beneficiaries had expressed about the adequacy of repair and maintenance services/other care. But 77 (42.77%) beneficiaries had expressed that the repair and maintenance service/other care were not adequate in their areas. All the 180 beneficiaries had expressed that there was no continuous support/guidance by the Govt. agencies on on-going basis. (Table 2A.18)

Beneficiaries had given various suggestions for improvement in the infrastructure facilities. The suggestions included development of road and electricity (by 108 beneficiaries), primary school with regular teachers (by 14 beneficiaries), opening of veterinary hospital (by 20 beneficiaries of Central Bihar), creation of purchase centre by 5 (2.77%) beneficiaries, control of recurring flood by 16 (8.88%) beneficiaries of North Bihar. 3 (1.6%) beneficiaries had given different suggestions whereas 2 (1.11%) had given no response (Table 2A.18).

The most shocking aspect about the performance of IRDP was that the schemes of 35 (19.44%) beneficiaries were non-

TABLE 2A.17

Training

Zone	Beneficiary Received any Training			Nature of Training					Utility of Training		
	Yes	No	Not required	Formal			Informal	N.A.	Useful	Not	N.A.
				TRYSEM	DWCRA	Any other					
North Bihar	00	60	00	00	00	00	00	00	00	00	00
Central Bihar	00	60	00	00	00	00	00	00	00	00	00
Jharkhand	09	05	46	01	00	00	08	00	08	01	00
Total	09	125	46	01	00	00	08	00	08	01	00

TABLE 2A.18

Linkage and after Care

Zone	Adequacy of Existing Infrastructure Facilities						Continued Support/ Guidance by Government Agencies on Going Basis		Beneficiary Suggestions to Improve Infrastructure Facilities							
	Availability of input		Marketing of output/ services		Availability of repair/ maintenance service/ other care											
	Yes	No	Yes	No	Yes	No	Yes	No	Road and Electricity	School with regular teacher	Veterinary hospital	Unit of dairy	Purchase centre	Cost of required food	Other	No response
North Bihar	58	02	56	04	55	05	00	60	29	07	00	00	01	16	00	07
Central Bihar	46	14	45	15	22	38	00	60	26	07	20	05	00	00	00	02
Jharkhand	33	27	47	13	26	34	00	60	53	00	00	00	04	00	03	00
Total	137	43	148	32	103	77	00	180	108	14	20	05	05	16	03	09

functional and schemes of 46 (25.5%) beneficiaries were only on paper, 19 (10.55%) beneficiaries had shown income from asset/ scheme upto Rs. 1000,41 (22.77%) in between Rs. 1001-2000, 24 (13.33%) in between Rs. 2001-3000, 8 (4.44%) in between Rs. 3001-4000, 5 (2.77%) in between Rs. 4001-5000. Only 2 (1.11%) beneficiaries of Central Bihar had shown their income in between Rs. 5001-6000. Not even a single beneficiary had shown income above Rs. 6000 per annum from the asset/ scheme. (Table 2A.19).

103 (57.22%) beneficiaries had faced obstacles in getting IRDP loan while 77 (42.77%) had not faced any obstacle. The main obstacle was procedural delay and payment of speed money. 98 (54.44%) beneficiaries had alleged about it. Only 5 (2.77%) beneficiaries had mentioned about obstacle created by middlemen. 48 (26.66%) beneficiaries out of 180 had awareness about group/cluster beneficiary approach of IRDP. But none had taken benefit of that approach. (Table 2A.20).

(c) General Observations and Recommendation

(i) Beneficiaries' Suggestions

23 (12.77%) beneficiaries had suggested that the beneficiary selection should be made through the credit camp. 85 (47.22%) beneficiaries had suggested that there must be a curb on speed money. They had suggested for procedural simplification and more transparency in the system. 5 (2.77%) beneficiaries had suggested that the interest should be charged from the beneficiaries after deducting the subsidy amount. Hence, no interest should be charged on the amount of subsidy, even if the subsidy amount would be adjusted at the time of final payment. 8 (4.44%) beneficiaries of Central Bihar had suggested that the law and order situation must be improved for the better performance of the scheme. They were facing severe problems like kidnapping of animals and assets and payment of ransom against that due to poor law and order situation. 6 (3.33%) beneficiaries had suggested that training must be an essential condition for selection of beneficiary. 12 (6.66%) beneficiaries had suggested that ceiling on loan amount for the scheme should be raised to undertake more viable schemes and generate viable income. 14 (7.77%) beneficiaries

Table 2A.19

Income from the Assets/Scheme

Zone	*1-1000*	*1001-2000*	*2001-3000*	*3001-4000*	*4001-5000*	*5001-6000*	*No Income as the Assets/Scheme was*	
							Not functional	*On paper only*
North Bihar	09	10	04	01	01	00	15	20
Central Bihar	07	12	05	03	00	02	13	18
Jharkhand	03	19	15	04	04	00	07	08
Total	19	41	24	08	05	02	35	46

TABLE 2A.20

General Observations

Zone	*Obstacles faced in getting IRDP Loan*		*Types of Obstacles*			*Awareness about Group/Cluster Beneficiary Approach of IRDP*		*Takn Benefit of Group/Cluster IRDP*	
	Yes	*No*	*Procedural delay and payment of speed money*	*Obstacles created by middle man*	*Any other*	*Yes*	*No*	*Yes*	*No*
North Bihar	32	28	32	00	00	06	54	00	60
Central Bihar	27	33	22	05	00	22	38	00	60
Jharkhand	44	16	44	00	00	20	40	00	60
Total	103	77	98	05	00	48	132	00	180

had given different suggestions while 27 (15.0%) had given no suggestion.

(ii) Investigators' Recommendations

Following were the recommendations of the investigators:

(1) Strict action should be taken for loan recovery to create seriousness about the scheme. Due to the loan waving schemes adopted by the Govt. in the past, most of the beneficiaries took loan not to create any viable income generating activity. They treated the entire loan amount as 100% subsidy.

(2) More openness and simplification in the procedure were essentially needed to curb the speed money in the system. Credit camps might help in this regard.

(3) Mass awareness campaign should be launched regarding the poverty alleviation programmes. Unfortunately common masses have little knowledge or no knowledge about the different dimensions of poverty alleviation programmes.

Investigators of North Bihar had recommended that effective steps should be taken to control the recurring flood problem, otherwise no viable scheme could be undertaken in the flood prone areas. They suggested that the pass book should be given to each and every beneficiary. They had identified that 20 schemes (33.3%) were completely fake. Beneficiaries had managed loan through payment of speed money not for the project but for the personal consumption. 15 (25.0%) schemes were not intact as the assets were perished. Only 25 (41.7%) schemes were genuine-schemes in the region.

Investigators of Central Bihar had further suggested that training should be essential condition for selection of beneficiaries. They had emphasised on strict law and order for proper utilization of the loan amount. They had identified that 18 schemes were completely fake, 12 schemes were non-functional as the assets were fully perished. Only 30 (50.0%) schemes were running as genuine schemes.

Investigators of Jharkhand had suggested that the loan

TABLE 2A.21

Policy Recommendations

Zone	*Beneficiary's Recommendations*								*Investigations observations & Recommendations*
	Selection/ loan through credit camp	*Curb on speed money and procedural simplification*	*Interest should be charged deducting the subsidy amount*	*Strict law and order*	*Training as an essential condition for beneficiary selections*	*Ceiling on loan amount be raised*	*Any other*	*No suggestion*	
1	*2*	*3*	*4*	*5*	*6*	*7*	*8*	*9*	*10*
North Bihar	13	24	01	00	03	06	00	13	Fake scheme -20 Not intact including perished -15 Genuine scheme -25 Recommendations : 1. Effective steps to control recurring flood 2. Loan pass book should be given 3. Strict action for loan recovery 4. Openness & simplification in the system and curb on speed money 5. Mass awareness campaign regarding poverty alleviation programmes

(Contd.)

TABLE 2A.21 *(Contd.)*

1	*2*	*3*	*4*	*5*	*6*	*7*	*8*	*9*	*10*
Central Bihar	03	23	04	08	03	05	14	00	Fake scheme -18 Not intact including perished -12 Genuine scheme -30 Recommendations : 1.Training should be essential condition for selection of beneficiary 2.Strict law and order 3. Strict action for loan recovery 4. Openness & simplification in the system and curb speed money 5. Mass awareness campaign regarding poverty alleviation programmes
South Bihar	07	38	00	00	00	01	00	14	Fake scheme -24 Not intact including perished -14 Genuine scheme -22 Recommendations : 1.Strict action for loan recovery 2. Openness & simplification in the system and curb on speed money 3. Mass awareness campaign regarding poverty alleviation programmes 4. Loan amount should be raised to undertake viable schemes
Total	23	85	05	08	06	12	14	27	

amount should be raised to undertake viable schemes to generate viable income to the beneficiaries. They identified that 24 schemes were completely fake. This proportion was higher even in comparison with North Bihar and Central Bihar. Assets of 14 schemes were not functional due to various reasons including the perished assets. Only 22 schemes were genuine and functional. This proportion was the lowest as 25 schemes were genuine in North Bihar and 30 schemes were genuine in Central Bihar. In brief only 77 (42.77%) schemes were functional and genuine of 180 schemes surveyed by the investigators.

(d) Calculation of Poverty Indices

Head-Count ratio (H)

$$H = \frac{q}{n},$$

where q = No. of beneficiaries below poverty line.
and n = Total number of beneficiaries.

$$= \frac{141}{180}$$

$$= 0.78$$

Income gap ratio (I)

$$I = \frac{g}{\pi . q},$$

where $g_i = \pi - y_i$ and $g = \sum_{i=1}^{n} g_i$

π = Poverty line Income.
Y_i = Income of ith beneficiary.

$$= \frac{1096700}{21000 \times 141}$$

$$= 0.37$$

Ginni Co-efficient (G)

$$G = \frac{\text{Area of shaded region in Fig. 2A.1}}{0.5}$$

$$\approx \frac{0.16}{0.50} \approx 0.32$$

Note: Fig 2A showing income inaquality for IRDP beneficiary attached herewith.

Now, Sen Index (P)

$$P = H \{I + (1\text{-}I)\ G\}$$

$$= 0.78\ \{0.37 + (1\text{-}0.37) \times 0.32\}$$

$$= 0.78\ \{0.37 + 0.63 \times 0.32\}$$

$$= 0.78\ \{0.37 + 0.20\}$$

$$= 0.78 \times 0.57$$

$$= 0.45$$

Note: The calculations have been made by approximating the values, upto two digits after decimal points.

An Analysis of Poverty Index for the scheme

The calculation of Head Count Ratio (H) shows that 78% of the beneficiaries were below poverty line. The value of Income Gap Ratio (I) comes out to be 0.37 which shows that most of the beneficiaries were in the upper income-slab below poverty line.

In the calculation of Sen-Index the value of Ginnie co-efficeint (G) is 0.32 which shows low degree of income disparity among the beneficiaries below poverty line. The value of Sen-Index (0.45) indicates that more beneficiaries were in the upper income-slab below poverty line, i.e., benefits are slightly skewed in favour of upper-income group below poverty line.

The Sen-Index value (0.45) gives a better picture as compared to Income gap ratio. This is due to the fact that the value of head-count ratio is much larger than the income-gap ratio.

FIG. 2A

Income Inequality for IRDP Beneficiaries

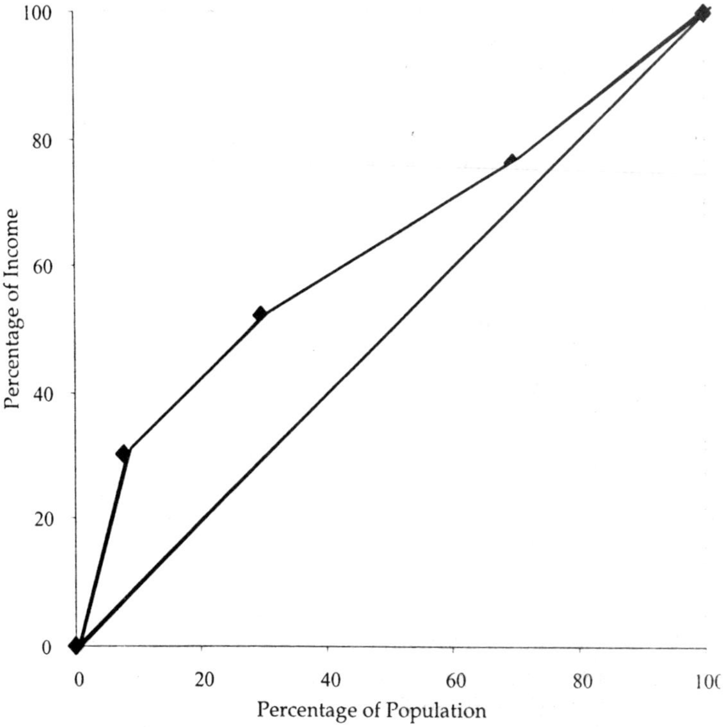

Percentage of Population	Percentage of Income
0	0
7.8	30.48
29.78	52.38
69.5	76.19
100	100

B. TRAINING OF RURAL YOUTH FOR SELF-EMPLOYMENT (TRYSEM)

The scheme - TRYSEM aimed at providing basic technical and entrepreneurial skill to the rural poor in the age group of 18-35 years enable them take up income generating activities (self/wage employment). It had been laid down that the coverage of youth from SC/ST communities should be at least 50% of rural youth trained. Out of the total beneficiaries, at least 50% should be women. The scheme had been merged into Swarnajayanti Gram Swarojgar Yojana (SGSY) with IRDP, DWCRA etc. from April, 1999.

(a) Socio-economic Condition of Beneficiary

Out of 60 beneficiaries, 49 (81.66%) were male and 11 (18.33%) were female. The least participation of women was prevalent in all the three sample zones, i.e, North Bihar, Central Bihar and Jharkhand.

56 (93.33%) beneficiaries were literate while only 4 (6.66%) were illiterate. Out of 56 literate persons. 35.71% had education below matriculation level, 50.0% had qualification of matriculation and above but below graduation level. And 14.28 % had qualification of graduation and above. Illiteracy level was comparatively higher in Jharkhand where 20.0% beneficiaries of the scheme were illiterate. And out of remaining 80.0% literate population 25.0% had only primary education, 35.0% had matriculation and above qualification but below the graduation level. 20.0% had graduation and above level.

Out of 60 beneficiaries, 20% were small farmers, 8.33% marginal farmers, only 6.66% were agricultural labourers, 8.33% non-agricultural casual labourers, 51.66% non-agricultural self-employed, 1.66% artisans and 3.33% were others.

Small farmers and non-agricultural self employed had taken the maximum benefit of the scheme. Marginal farmers had taken the benefits of the scheme only in Central Bihar zone, where only 5 beneficiaries (8.33% of the beneficiaries of the zone) were marginal farmers (Table 2B.1)

36.66% beneficiaries had the family size of 1-5 persons, 58.33% had of 6-11 persons and only 5.0% had the family size of 12 or more. Hence only 3 beneficiaries (5.0%) belonged to

TABLE 2B.1

Categorisation of Beneficiaries

Zone	Sex		Literacy		Literacy Level			Beneficiary's Occupation at the Time of Selection						
	Male	Female	Literate	Illiterate	Primary & above	Matric & above	Graduation & above	SF	MF	Agri-Labour	Non-agri. Casual Labour	Non-agri. Self employed	Artisan	Others
North Bihar	20	00	20	00	11	08	01	04	00	01	00	15	00	00
Central Bihar	16	04	20	00	04	13	03	06	05	03	04	01	01	00
Jharkhand	13	07	16	04	05	07	04	02	00	00	01	15	00	02
Total	49	11	56	04	20	28	08	12	05	04	05	31	01	02

combined family. The trend was almost similar in all the three sample zones.

34 (56.66%) beneficiaries belonged to schedules castes and 19 (31.66%) belonged to OBCs. Only 2 (3.33%) beneficiaries belonged to scheduled tribes and 5 (8.33%) belonged to other caste groups including minorities. Hence SCs had taken the maximum benefit of the IRDP followed by OBC groups.

Priority under the scheme was to be given to the freed bonded labourers and assignees of surplus land. But only 1 (1.66%) beneficiary was freed bonded labour and even not a single beneficiary was the assignee of surplus land. Remaining 59 (98.33%) belonged to other categories (Table 2B.2)

Not even a single beneficiary of the scheme had income below Rs. 6401. 7 (11.66%) beneficiaries had income in between Rs. 6401-11000, 7 (11.66%) beneficiaries had income in between Rs. 11001-16000 and 14 (23.33%) beneficiaries in between Rs. 16001-21000. 19 (31.66%) beneficiaries had income above Rs. 21000 but below Rs. 32000. And 13 (21.66%) beneficiaries had income above Rs. 32000. Hence 32 (53.33%) beneficiaries did not come under the purview of the scheme as their income level was above the poverty line but they managed to take the benefit of the scheme. Hence, manipulation by the better-off section was apparent in the scheme (Table 2B.3)

(b) Economic Structure and Viability of the Scheme

50 (83.33%) beneficiaries had taken training under the scheme of 6 months duration while 10 (16.66%) beneficiaries of Jharkhand region had taken training in course of 3 months duration. Beneficiaries had taken training in different types of courses including typing, bidi binding, pumpset repairing, electrical works, sheet metal, grill welder, radio mechanic, veterinary compounder, tractor repairing, motor driving readymade garments and carpentry etc.

Unfortunately only 18 (30.0%) beneficiaries had accepted that the course had helped them in skill formation in the training area while 42 (70.0%) beneficiaries opined that the course could not help them in skill formation. Only 4 (6.66%) beneficiaries had shown full satisfaction about the course. 13 (21.66%) beneficiaries had shown simple satisfaction while 3 (5.0%) had shown less satisfaction. 40 (66.6%) beneficiaries had

TABLE 2B.2

Size of the Family and Social Classification

Zone	Size of the Family			Social Classification						
				Category I				Category II		
	1-5	6-11	12+	SC	ST	OBCs	Others	Ex/freed bonded labour	Assignies of surplus land	Others
North Bihar	03	15	02	09	00	06	05	00	00	20
Central Bihar	09	10	01	14	00	06	00	01	00	19
Jharkhand	10	10	00	11	02	07	00	00	00	20
Total	22	35	03	34	02	19	05	01	00	59

TABLE 2B.3

Family Income

Zone	*Below Poverty Line*			*Above Poverty Line*		
	Upto 6400	*6401-11000*	*11001-16000*	*16001-21000*	*21001-32000*	*32001+*
North Bihar	00	00	01	04	07	08
Central Bihar	00	00	02	06	07	05
Jharkhand	00	07	04	04	05	00
Total	00	07	07	14	19	13

described the course was completely unsatisfactory. 24 (40.0%) beneficiaries had alleged that not the trainers were competent. That was the reason of unsatisfactory performance. 11 (18.33%) beneficiaries had alleged that lack of seriousness amongst authorities including trainers was the reason of unsatisfactory performance. 2 (3.33%) beneficiaries had alleged that the scheme was only a paper work. Only 3 (5.0%) beneficiaries had accepted that they could not take the benefit of the course due to their engagement in some other work. Hence they did not have any idea about the course. (Table 2B.4)

Only 1 (1.66%) beneficiary had claimed that he was selected for the training on the basis of merit. 24 (40.0%) beneficiaries were selected with the help of block authorities, 4 (6.66%) with the help of Panchayat authority and 10 (16.66%) with the help of other influential persons. 21 (35.0%) beneficiaries reported that due to mass unawareness about the scheme, there was easy access. The actual amount of stipend was Rs. 350 per month but 7 (11.66%) beneficiaries had not received any amount. 3 (5.0%) beneficiaries had received in between Rs 1-500, 9 (15.0%) in between Rs. 501-1000, 18 (30.0%) in between Rs. 1001-1500, and 23 (38.33%) in between Rs. 1501-2000. Not even a single beneficiary had received full stipend amount. 33 (55.0%) beneficiaries had alleged that the remaining stipend amounts were appropriated by Block authorities. 5 (8.33%) reported that remaining amounts were appropriated by the middlemen whereas 22 (36.66%) beneficiaries had no idea. (Table 2B.5)

TABLE 2B.4

Satisfaction about the Course

Zone	Duration of Course	Type of the Course							Skill Formation in the Training Area		Satisfaction Base				Reason for Unsatisfactory Performance				
		Tailoring	Bidi making	Colour printing	Bangle making	Ready made garments	Carpet making	Murtikala	Yes	No	Fully Satisfactory	Satisfactory	Less satisfactory	Unsatisfactory	Only paper work	Trainers not competent	Lack of seriousness	Beneficiary engagement in some other work	Any other
North Bihar	6 months	04	03	03	10	00	00	00	13	07	05	07	00	08	00	05	02	01	00
Central Bihar	6 months	00	00	00	00	10	10	00	13	07	00	02	01	17	06	05	05	01	00
Jharkhand	6 months	10	00	00	00	00	00	10	06	14	00	13	04	03	00	01	01	01	00
Total		14	03	03	10	10	10	10	32	28	05	22	05	28	06	11	08	03	00

TABLE 2B.5

Beneficiary Selection and Stipend

Zone	Selection of Beneficiary of the Basis of						Stipend Amount Actual payment						Full Stipend Amount Received		In Case of Partial Stipend Payent or No Payment the Rest Amount Appropriated by		
	Merit test	Help of block authority	Help of panchayat authority	Help of influential person	Easy access due to mass unawareness	As per scheme (Rs. per months)	0	0-500	501-1000	1001-1500	1501-2000	2001+	Yes	No	Block authority	Middle man	No idea
North Bihar	00	10	01	01	08	350	05	03	00	09	03	00	00	20	10	00	10
Central Bihar	01	03	03	07	06	350	01	00	00	09	10	00	00	20	03	05	12
Jharkhand	00	11	00	02	07	350	01	00	09	00	10	00	00	20	20	00	00
Total	01	24	04	10	21		07	03	09	18	23	00	00	60	33	05	22

Out of 60, only 15 (25.0%) beneficiaries reported that they had been benefitted by the training. 2 (3.33%) had got benefit in getting job on the basis of training, 10 (16.66%) had enhanced their productivity level under self employment activity, 2 (3.33%) had enhanced their quality level under self-employment activities and 1 (1.66%) had received loan under self employment scheme due to the training, but 45 (75.0%) beneficiaries reported that they had not received any benefit due to the training/scheme. Out of 60, only 2 (3.33%) beneficiaries had received IRDP loan. 24 (40.0%) had not applied for the IRDP loan because they had no idea that the training would facilitate them in getting IRDP loan. 34 (56.66%) TRYSEM beneficiaries had applied for the loan but couldn't get due to the procedural obstacles and corruption. The trend was similar in all the three zones. (Table 2B.6)

Out of 60 beneficiaries, only 15 (25.0%) were engaged in the training area. 13 (86.6%) amongst them had accepted that their income levels had been raised due to their engagement in training area. 42 (70.0%) beneficiaries were working in self employment scheme whereas 18 (30.0%) beneficiaries in wage employment scheme. (Table 2B.7)

(c) General Observations and Recommendations

Beneficiaries of the scheme had given the following broad observations :

(i) The trainers of the schemes were serious not to impart knowledge to the beneficiaries but to fulfil the formalities.

(ii) Training centres were mismanaged and ill-equipped.

(iii) Full stipend amounts were not paid and the remaining amounts in sizeable proportion were appropriated by authorities.

(iv) Amount of purchasing raw materials for the training was fully appropriated by the authorities.

(v) No training certificate was issued to the beneficiaries.

TABLE 2B.6

Benefit for the Scheme

Zone	*Type of Benefit from Training*					*Received IRDP Loan on the Basis of Training*		*Reason for not Receiving TRDP Loan Inspite of Training Procedural*		
	New Job assign-ment	*Enhance-ment of productivity level under self-employ-ment*	*Enhance-ment in the quality level under self-employ-ment*	*Receiving loan under self-employ-ment scheme*	*No Benefit*	*Yes*	*No*	*Not applied*	*Proced-ural obstacles/ corruption*	*Any other*
North Bihar	00	00	00	00	20	00	20	10	10	00
Central Bihar	02	01	02	00	15	02	18	09	09	00
Jharkhand	00	09	00	01	10	00	20	05	15	00
Total	02	10	02	01	45	02	58	24	34	00

TABLE 2B.7

Use of the Scheme and General Observations

Zone	*Beneficiary Engaged in Training Area*		*Income Level has been raised due to Beneficiary's Engaged in Training Area*		*Benficiary is Working*		*Beneficiary's Observation*	*Investigator's Observation*
	Yes	*No*	*Yes*	*No*	*Self employ-ment scheme*	*Wage employ-ment scheme*		
North Bihar	00	20	00	20	20	00	1. Trainers were serious not to impart knowledge to the beneficiaries, but to fulfil the formalities.	1. The scheme has been undertaken by the management/trainers only to complete the formalities by fulfilling the paper works.
Central Bihar	05	15	04	16	14	06	2. Training centres were mismanaged and illless equipped.	2. Beneficiaries also failed to unde-rstand the importance of the scheme. Recommendations :
Jharkhand	10	10	09	11	08	12	3. Full stipend amounts were not paid and the remaining amounts were appropriated by the authorities.	1. Effective steps should be taken for providing adequate snacks and lunch to the beneficiary during the training period in addition to their full stipend amount.

Total	15	45	13	47	42	18	4. Amount for purchase of raw materials for training was fully appropriated by the authorities. 5. No certificate was issued to the beneficiaries.	2. Beneficaries should be supplied full information about the course including the duration stipend amount and the amount of raw materials for training. 3. Training should be made an essential condition for getting financial assistance under SGSY. 4. Training centres should be well managed and equipped with the competent trainers.

Investigators observations and recommendations

On the basis of cross-survey the investigators confirmed that the scheme had been undertaken by the management and trainers only to complete the formalities by fulfilling the paper works. They had also observed that the beneficiaries were not very serious about the course as they couldn't understand the importance of the scheme. They had given the following recommendations :

(i) Effective steps should be taken for providing adequate snacks and lunch to the beneficiaries against their full stipend amounts. It might create an additional interest in the course.

(ii) Training should be made an essential condition for getting financial assistance under SGSY.

(iii) Beneficiaries should be supplied full information about the course including the duration stipend amount and the amount allocated for the purchase of raw materials for training.

(iv) Training centres should be well managed and well equipped with competent trainers.

(d) Calculation of Poverty Indices

Head-Count ratio (H)

$$H = \frac{q}{n} = \frac{28}{60} = 0.46$$

Income - gap ratio

$$I = \frac{g}{\pi . q}$$

$$= \frac{181200}{21000 \times 28}$$

$$= 0.3081632$$

Ginni Co-efficient (G)
G = 0.20

Now, Sen Index (P)

P= H [I + (1-I) G]

= 0.46 [0.31 + (1-0.31) x 0.20]

= 0.46 [0.31 + 0.69) x 0.20]

= 0.46 [0.32 + 0.138]

= 0.46 x 0.448

= 0.21

C. DEVELOPMENT OF WOMEN AND CHILDREN IN RURAL AREAS (DWCRA)

The scheme - DWCRA was aimed to improve the socio-economic status of the poor women in the rural areas through creation of groups of women for income-generating activities on a self-sustaining basis. The main strategy adopted under the programme was to facilitate access for poor women to employment, skill upgradation, training credit and other support services so that the DWCRA women as a group could take up income-generating activities for supplementing their incomes. It sought to encourage collective action in the form of group activities which were known to work better and were more sustainable than the individual effort. It encouraged the habit of thrift and credit among poor rural women to make them self-reliant.

The Scheme had been merged into Swarnajayanti Gram Swarojgar Yojana (SGSY) with IRDP, TRYSEM etc. from April, 1999.

(a) Socio-economic Condition of Beneficiary

Out of all the 60 female beneficiaries, 40 (66.66%) were literate and 20 (33.33%) were illiterate. Out of 40 literate beneficiaries, 38 (95.0%) had education below matriculation level, only 5% (2) had qualification of matriculation and above but below graduation level whereas no beneficiary could reach

FIG. 2B

Income Inequality for TRYSEM Beneficiaries

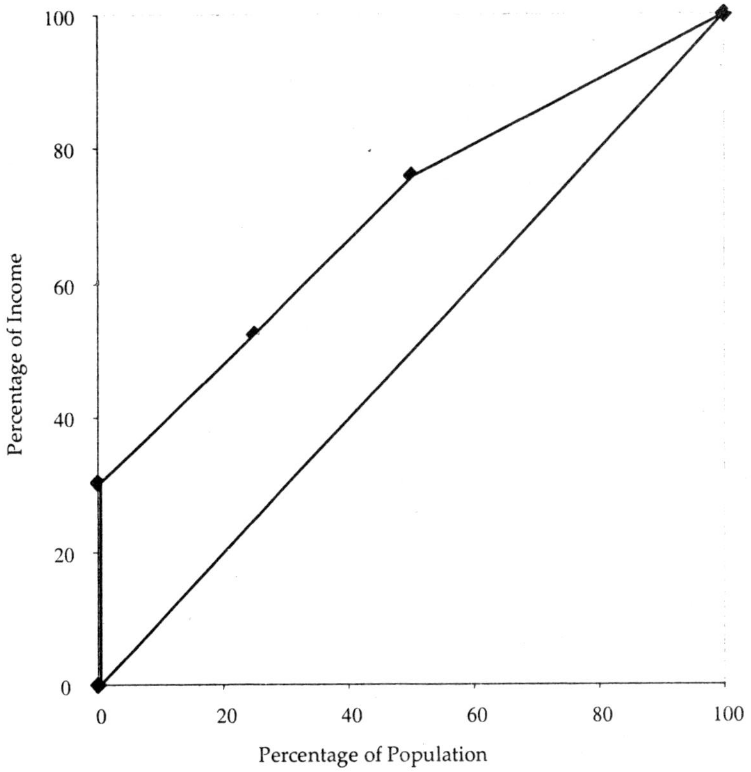

Percentage of Population	Percentage of Income
0	0
0	30.48
25	52.38
50	76.19
100	100

upto graduation level. Illiteracy level was higher in Central Bihar zone where 70% (14) beneficiaries of the scheme were illiterate. And out of remaining 30.0% (6) literate population, 83.33% (5) had only primary education, 16.66% (1) had matriculation and above qualification but below the graduation level.

Out of 60 beneficiaries only 3 (5.0%) were small farmers, 18 (30.0%) were agricultural labourers only 6 (10%) were non-agricultural casual labourers, 20 (33.33%) were non-agricultural self-employed, only 3 (5.0%) were artisans and 10 (16.66%) were others including house wives. Agricultural labourers and non-agricultural self employed had taken the maximum benefit of the scheme. Non-agricultural labourers had taken the benefit only in Jharkhand region, where 100.0% beneficiaries were non agricultural labourers (Table 2C.1).

51.66% beneficiaries had the family size of 1-5 members, 46.66% had the size of 6-11 members and only 1.66% had the family size of 12 or more. Hence only 1 beneficiary belonged to the combined family. The trend was almost similar in all the three zones.

24 (40.0%) beneficiaries belonged to scheduled castes, 30 (50.0%) belonged to OBCs and 6 (10%) beneficiaries only from North Bihar belonged to other caste groups including minorities.

Priority under the scheme was to be given to the freed bonded labourers and assignees of surplus land. But only 03 (5.0%) beneficiaries were freed bonded labourers and even not a single beneficiary was the assignee of surplus land. Remaining 57 (95%) belonged to other categories. (Table 2C.2)

Not even a single beneficiary of the scheme had income below Rs. 6401. 9 (15.0%) beneficiaries had income in between Rs. 6401-11000, 21 (35.0%) in between Rs. 11001-16000 and 13 (21.66%) in between Rs. 16001-21000. 13 (21.66%) also in between Rs. 21001-32000 and 4 (6.66%) beneficiaries had income above Rs. 32000. Hence 17 (28.32%) beneficiaries did not come under the purview of scheme as their income level was above the poverty line but they managed to take the benefit of the scheme. Hence, manipulation by the better-off section was apparent in the scheme. (Table 2C.3)

TABLE 2C.1

Categorisation of Beneficiaries

Zone	*Sex*		*Literacy*		*Literacy Level*			*Beneficiary's Occupation at the Time of Selection*						
	Male	*Female*	*Literate*	*Illiterate*	*Primary & above*	*Matric & above*	*Graduation & above*	*SF*	*MF*	*Agri-Labour*	*Non-agri. Casual Labour*	*Non-agri. Self employed*	*Artisan*	*Others*
North Bihar	00	20	17	03	17	00	00	00	00	01	00	09	00	10
Central Bihar	00	20	06	14	05	01	00	01	00	16	00	03	00	00
Jharkhand	00	20	17	03	16	01	00	02	00	01	06	08	03	00
Total	00	60	40	20	38	02	00	03	00	18	06	20	03	10

TABLE 2C.2

Size of the Family and Social Classification

Zone	*Size of the Family*			*Social Classification*						
				Category I				*Category II*		
	1-5	*6-11*	*12+*	*SC*	*ST*	*OBCs*	*Others*	*Ex/freed bonded labour*	*Assignies of surplus land*	*Others*
North Bihar	10	10	00	03	00	11	06	00	00	20
Central Bihar	11	08	01	19	00	01	00	03	00	17
Jharkhand	10	10	00	02	00	18	00	00	00	20
Total	31	28	01	24	00	30	06	03	00	57

TABLE 2C.3

Family Income

Zone	Below Poverty Line			Above Poverty Line		
	Upto 6400	6401- 11000	11001- 16000	16001- 21000	21001- 32000	32001+
North Bihar	00	00	06	04	08	02
Central Bihar	00	04	07	04	03	02
Jharkhand	00	05	08	05	02	00
Total	00	09	21	13	13	04

(b) Economic Structure and Viability of the Scheme

60 (100.0%) beneficiaries had taken training under the scheme of 6 months duration.

Beneficiaries had taken training in different types of courses including typing, bidi binding, pumpset, repairing electrical works, sheet metal, grill welder, radio mechanic, veterinary compounder, tractor repairing, motor driving, readymade garments, and carpentry etc.

Only 32 (53.33%) beneficiaries had accepted that the course had helped them in skill formation in the training area while 28 (46.66%) beneficiaries had opined that the course could not help them in skill formation. Only 5 (8.33%) beneficiaries had shown full satisfaction about the course. 22 (36.66%) beneficiaries had shown simple satisfaction while 5 (8.33%) had shown less satisfaction. 28 (46.66%) beneficiaries had described the course completely unsatisfactory. 11 (18.33%) beneficiaries had alleged that the trainers were not competent. That was the reason of unsatisfactory performance. 8 (13.33%) beneficiaries had alleged that lack of seriousness, amongst authorities including trainers was the reason of unsatisfactory performance. 6 (10.0%) beneficiaries had alleged that the scheme was only a paper work. Only 3 (5.0%) beneficiaries accepted that they could not take the benefit of the course due to their engagements in some other work. Hence, they had no idea about the course. (Table - 2CA)

Not a single beneficiary had claimed that he/she was selected for the training on the basis of merit. 33 (55.0%)

TABLE 2C.4

Satisfaction about the Course

Zone	Duration of Course	Type of the Course							Skill Formation in the Training Area		Satisfaction Base				Reason for Unsatisfactory Performance				
		Tailoring	Bidi making	Colour printing	Bangle making	Ready made garments	Carpet making	Murtikala	Yes	No	Fully Satisfactory	Satisfactory	Less satisfactory	Unsatisfactory	Only paper work	Trainers not competent	Lack of seriousness	Beneficiary engagement in some other work	Any other
North Bihar	6 months	04	03	03	10	00	00	00	13	07	05	07	00	08	00	05	02	01	00
Central Bihar	6 months	00	00	00	00	10	10	00	13	07	00	02	01	17	06	05	05	01	00
Jharkhand	6 months	10	00	00	00	00	00	10	06	14	00	13	04	03	00	01	01	01	00
Total		14	03	03	10	10	10	10	32	28	05	22	05	28	06	11	08	03	00

beneficiaries were selected with the help of block authorities, 3 (5.0%) with the help of Panchayat authority and 23 (38.33%) with the help of other influential persons. Only 1 (1.66%) beneficiary had reported that due to mass unawareness about the scheme, there was easy access. The actual amount of stipend was Rs. 350/- per month but 20 (33.33%) beneficiaries had not received any amount. Not a single beneficiary was there who had received Rs. 1-500. 10 (16.66%) had received in between Rs. 501-1000, 10 (16.66%) in between Rs. 1001-1500, 20 (33.33%) in between Rs. 1501-2000. Not even a single beneficiary had received full stipend amount. 32 (53.33%) beneficiaries had alleged that the remaining stipend amounts were appropriated by the Block authorities. 5 (8.33%) reported that remaining amounts were appropriated by the middlemen whereas 23 (38.33%) beneficiaries had no idea (Table 2C.5)

Out of 60, only 9 (15.0%) beneficiaries had reported that they had been benefitted by the training. Not even a single beneficiary had got benefit in getting job on the basis of training, only 2 (3.33%) had enhanced their productivity level under self-employment activity, 04 (6.66%) had enhanced their quality level under self-employment activities and 3 (5.0%) had received loan under self-employment scheme due to the training, but 51 (58.0%) beneficiaries reported that they had not received any benefit due to the training/scheme. Out of 60, only 3 (5.0%) beneficiaries had received IRDP loan, 24 (40.0%) had not applied for the IRDP loan because they had no idea that the training would facilitate them in getting IRDP loan.

34 (56.66%) DWCRA beneficiaries had applied for the loan but couldn't get due to the procedural obstacles and corruption. The trend was similar in all the three zones (Table 2C.6)

Out of 60 beneficiaries, only 9 (15.0%) were engaged in the training area. Only 8 (13.33%) amongst them had accepted that their income levels had been raised due to their engagement in training area. 32 (53.33%) beneficiaries were working in self employment scheme whereas 18 (30.0%) beneficiaries in wage employment scheme. (Table 2C.7).

(c) General Observations and Recommendations

Beneficiaries of the scheme had given the following broad observations :

TABLE 2C.5

Beneficiary Selection and Stipend

Zone	Selection of Beneficiary of the Basis of						Stipend Amount Actual payment						Full Stipend Amount Received		In Case of Partial Stipend Payent or No Payment the Rest Amount Appropriated by		
	Merit test	*Help of block authority*	*Help of panchayat authority*	*Help of influential person*	*Easy access due to mass unawareness*	*As per scheme (Rs. per months)*	*0*	*0-500*	*501-1000*	*1001-1500*	*1501-2000*	*2001+*	*Yes*	*No*	*Block authority*	*Middle man*	*No idea*
North Bihar	00	17	00	02	01	00	00	00	10	10	00	00	00	20	15	02	03
Central Bihar	00	02	03	15	00	00	20	00	00	00	00	00	00	20	00	00	20
Jharkhand	00	14	00	06	00	350	00	00	00	00	20	00	00	20	17	03	00
Total	00	33	03	23	01	350	20	00	10	10	20	00	00	60	32	05	23

TABLE 2C.6

Benefit for the Scheme

Zone	*Type of Benefit from Training*					*Received IRDP Loan on the Basis of Training*		*Reason for not Receiving TRDP Loan Inspite of Training Procedural*		
	New Job assign-ment	*Enhance-ment of productivity level under self-employ-ment*	*Enhance-ment in the quality level under self-employ-ment*	*Receiving loan under self-employ-ment scheme*	*No Benefit*	*Yes*	*No*	*Not applied*	*Proced-ural obstacles/ corruption*	*Any other*
North Bihar	00	00	00	00	20	00	20	10	10	00
Central Bihar	00	00	03	00	17	02	18	13	05	00
Jharkhand	00	02	01	03	14	01	19	01	19	00
Total	00	02	04	03	51	03	57	24	34	00

TABLE 2C.7

Use of the Scheme and General Observations

Zone	*Beneficiary Engaged in Training Area*		*Income Level has been raised due to Beneficiary's Engaged in Training Area*		*Income Level has not been Raised Inspite of Beneficiary's Engagement in Training Area due to*	*Benficiary is Working*			*Beneficiary's Observation*	*Investigator's Observation*
	Yes	*No*	*Yes*	*No*		*Self employment scheme*	*Wage employment scheme*	*Housewife*		
North Bihar	00	20	00	20	—	19	01	00	1. Full stipend amount was not paid and the remaining amount was appropriated by the authorities	1. A sizeable proportion of stipend amount was appropriated by the authorities. 100% incase of Central Bihar.
Central Bihar	03	17	03	17	—	07	13	00	2. Amount for purchase of raw materials for beneficiaries was fully appropriated by	2. Amount for purchase of raw materials was fully appropriated by the authorities.

									the authorities	Recommendations :
Jharkhand	06	14	05	15	lack of working capital	06	04	10	3. No certificate was issued to the beneficiaries. 4. No follow-up action was taken to induce the beneficiary to continue in the training area.	1. Level of training centres and trainers should be improved to make the scheme more effective and purposive. 2. Follow-up action is needed to induce the beneficiaries to continue in the training area.
Total	09	51	08	52	—	32	18	10		3. Full information about the course should be supplied to the beneficiaries including course duration, stipend amount and amount allocated for purchase of raw materials.

(i) Full stipend amount was not paid and the remaining amount was appropriated by the authorities.
(ii) The amount for purchase of raw materials for beneficiaries was fully appropriated by the authorities.
(iii) Even no certificate was issued to the beneficiaries.
(iv) No follow-up action was taken to include the beneficiary to continue in the training areas.

Investigators Observations and Recommendations

On the basis of cross-survey the Investigators have confirmed that a sizeable proportion of stipend amount was appropriated by the authorities, 100% in case of Central Bihar.

In addition, amount for purchase of raw materials was fully appropriated by the authorities.

They had given the following recommendations :

(i) Level of training centres and trainers should be improved to make the scheme more effective and purposive.
(ii) Follow-up action must be needed to induce the beneficiaries to continue in the training areas.
(iii) Full information about the course should be given to the beneficiaries including course duration, stipend amount allocated for purchase of raw materials.

(d) Calculation of Poverty Indices

Head-Count ratio :

$$H = \frac{q}{n} = \frac{43}{60} = 0.716$$

Income - Gap ratio :

$$I = \frac{g}{\pi . q} = \frac{291000}{21000 \times 43} = 0.322$$

Ginni Co-efficient (G)

G = 0.17

Sen - Index (P)

Now, Sen Index (P)

$P = H [I + (1-I) G]$

$= 0.72 [0.32 + (1-0.32) \times 0.17]$

$= 0.72 [0.32 + 0.68) \times 0.17]$

$= 0.72 [0.32 + 0.11]$

$= 0.72 \times 0.43$

$= 0.31$

An Analysis of Povety Index for the Scheme

The estimated value of the Head-Count Ratio (H) shows that approximately 72% of the beneficiaries were below poverty line. The computed value of Income-Gap Ratio (I) viz. 0.32 shows that a considerable number of beneficiaries were in the upper income-slab below poverty line.

The calculaiton of Sen-Index, the value of Ginni co-efficeint (G) is 0.17. This shows a low degree of income disparity among the beneficiaries below poverty line.

The value of Sen-Index -0.31 signifies that a large number of beneficiaries were in the upper income-slab below poverty line, i.e., benefits being skewed in favour of upper income-slab below poverty line.

FIG. 2C

Income Inequality for DWCRA Beneficiaries

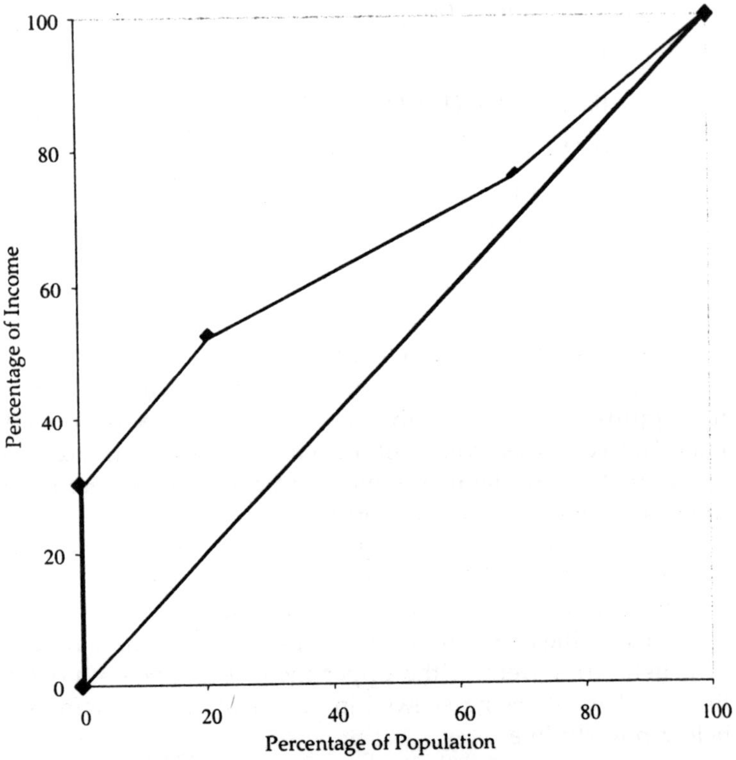

Percentage of Population	Percentage of Income
0	0
0	30.48
20.93	52.38
69.76	76.19
100	100

CHAPTER

3

WAGE EMPLOYMENT PROGRAMMES

A. JAWAHAR GRAM SAMRIDHI YOJANA (JGSY)/ JAWAHAR ROJGAR YOJANA (JRY)

JRY was launched as a centrally sponsored scheme on April 1st, 1989 by merging the National Rural Employment Programme (NREP) and Rural Landless Employment Guarantee Programme (RLEGP). The main objective of the programme was the generation of additional gainful employment for unemployed and under employed men and women in rural areas through creation of rural economic infrastructure, community and social assets. The resources under the scheme were allocated to the states/UTs on the basis of proportion of rural poor in the states/UTs to the total rural poor in the country.

The programme was targetted at people living below poverty line with preference to SCs/STs and freed bonded labourers. At least 30% employment was to be provided to women under the scheme. Works under the scheme could be taken up during any part of the year as per the felt need for employment generation preferably during the lean agricultural season but could be continued thereafter as per the necessity. In the year 1993-94 the 2nd stream of JRY was introduced in 120 identified backward districts in 12 states of the country with a target of providing 90-100 days of employment per person in backward districts where there was a concentration of unemployed and underemployed persons. In addition, a 3rd stream was introduced for taking up special and innovative projects aimed at preventing migration of labourers, enhancing women's employment and undertaking special programmes through voluntary organisations for drought proofing too.

In a comprehensive restructuring of the wage employment programmes on 1.1.1996, JRY was further streamlined. In the revised strategy, the first stream of JRY was continued in the existing form but Indira Awaas Yojana (IAY) and Million Wells Scheme (MWS), which were till then the sub-schemes of JRY, were made independent schemes. The 2nd stream of JRY, which was being implemented in 120 backward districts in the country, was merged with the Employment Assurance Scheme (EAS) introduced in 1775 selected backward blocks of the country in 1993-94 in view of the similarity in these programmes. The 3rd stream of JRY with its thrust on innovative projects was continued. Accordingly, the JRY was being implemented in two parts : (i) the Jawahar Rozgar Yojana (Main Scheme), and (ii) Special and innovative Projects.

JRY had been restructured and streamlined with effect from April, 1999 and had been renamed as JGSY. The Primary objective of JGSY is the creation of demand driven village infrastructure including durable assets at the village level to enable the rural poor to increase the opportunity for sustained employment. The secondary objective is the generation of supplementary employment for the unemployed poor in the rural areas while there is no sectoral earmarking of resources under JGSY, 22.5% of the annual allocation must be spent on beneficiary schemes for scheduled castes/scheduled tribes and 3% of annual allocation is to be utilised for the creation of barrier-free infrastructure for the disabled. Another objective is to generate supplementary employment for the unemployed rural poor.

The study had evaluated the performance of JRY - one of the main scheme for wage employment with an objective to suggest viable measures for successful implementation of JGSY.

(a) Socio-economic Condition of the Beneficiaries

Out of 180 beneficiaries, 177 (98.33%) were male and only

3 (1.67%) were female, 100% beneficiaries of North Bihar and Jharkhand were male and only 5.0% of the beneficiaries of Central Bihar were female. It indicated the insignificant participation of women in the scheme which was completely against the target.

45.0% beneficiaries were literate while 55.0% were illiterate. Out of 45.0% literate population, 37.2% had education below matriculation level and 7.77% had qualification of matriculation and above but below graduation level. Illiteracy level was higher in North Bihar where 76.66% of the beneficiaries were illiterate. And out of 23.34% literate population, 18.33% had only primary education, only 5.0% had matriculation and above qualification but below graduation level. Central Bihar and Jharkhand were better placed.

Out of 180 beneficiaries, 9.44% were small farmers, 3.88% were marginal farmers, 48.88% were agricultural labourers, 21.66% were non-agricultural casual labourers, 6.66% were non-agricultural self-employed, 6.66% were artisans and 2.77% were others. Agricultural labourers had taken maximum benefit of the scheme in North Bihar and Central Bihar where the proportion was 85.0% and 48.3% respectively. Non-agricultural labourers had taken the benefit of the scheme in Jharkhand where the proportion was 51.66% out of the total beneficiaries of the region. (Table 3A.1)

43.88% beneficiaries had the family size of 1-5 persons, 51.66% beneficiaries had the family size of 6-11 persons and only 4.44% beneficiaries had the family size of 12 or more. Hence only 8 (4.44%) beneficiaries belonged to combined family. Not even a single beneficiary of Jharkhand came in this category. 81 (45.0%) beneficiaries belonged to SCs and 99 (55.0%) belonged to OBCs. Only 1.11% of the beneficiaries belonged to freed bonded labour category and 2.77% were assignees of surplus land. Remaining 173 (96.11%) belonged to other categories (Table 3A.2).

Only 1 beneficiary had income in between Rs. 6401-11000. 30 (16.66%) had income in between Rs. 11001-16000, 109 (60.55%) in between Rs. 16001-21000, surprisingly 29 (16.11%) beneficiaries had income in between Rs. 21001-32000 and 11 (6.11%) beneficiaries had income above Rs. 32000. Hence, 40 (22.22%) beneficiaries did not come under the purview of the

TABLE 3A.1

Categorisation of Beneficiaries

Zone	Sex		Literacy		Literacy Level			Beneficiary's Occupation at the Time of Selection						
	Male	Female	Literate	Illiterate	Primary & above	Matric & above	Graduation & above	SF	MF	Agri-Labour	Non-agri. Casual Labour	Non-agri. Self employed	Artisan	Others
North Bihar	60	00	14	46	11	03	00	01	00	51	08	00	00	00
Central Bihar	57	03	36	24	27	09	00	08	07	29	00	05	11	00
Jharkhand	60	00	31	29	29	02	00	08	00	08	31	07	01	05
Total	177	03	81	99	67	14	00	17	07	88	39	12	12	05

TABLE 3A.2

Size of the Family and Social Classification

Zone	*Size of the Family*			*Social Classification*						
				Category I				*Category II*		
	1-5	*6-11*	*12+*	*SC*	*ST*	*OBCs*	*Others*	*Ex/freed bonded labour*	*Assignies of surplus land*	*Others*
North Bihar	23	36	01	45	00	15	00	00	05	55
Central Bihar	26	27	07	33	00	27	00	02	00	58
Jharkhand	30	30	00	03	00	57	00	00	00	60
Total	79	93	08	81	00	99	00	02	05	173

scheme on the basis of their income. Not a single beneficiary of Jharkhand had income above Rs. 32000. (Table 3 A. 3)

TABLE 3A.3

Family Income

Zone	*Below Poverty Line*			*Above Poverty Line*		
	Upto 6400	*6401- 11000*	*11001- 16000*	*16001- 21000*	*21001- 32000*	*32001+*
North Bihar	00	00	11	38	09	02
Central Bihar	00	01	11	31	08	09
Jharkhand	00	00	08	40	12	00
Total	00	01	30	109	29	11

(b) Economic Structure and Viability of the Scheme

118 (65.5%) beneficiaries reported that the selection of works was made on the recommendation of the Gram Sabha. 27 (15.0%) reported that works were selected directly by the block office, 35 (19.44%) reported that works were selected on the recommendation of influential persons including contractors.

3 (1.66%) beneficiaries had received information about the JRY from V.L.W., 50 (27.77%) had received information through friends, 120 (66.66%) from contractors and 7 (3.88%) from other sources. 2 (1.11%) beneficiaries were selected for the works on the recommendation of V.L.W., 12 (6.66%) on the recommendation of influential persons, 162 (90.0%) on the recommendation of contractors and 4 (2.22%) on the recommendation of others. Hence, dominant role of contractors were well established in all the three zones. (Table 3A.4)

163 (90.55%) beneficiaries had opined that the selections of works were made on the felt need of the people. 120 (66.66%) had received work under the scheme due to the proximity with the contractors, 46 (25.55%) had received work by doing extra work for someone, 1 (0.55%) received work by paying some money and 13 (7.22%) through other sources. 35 (19.44%) beneficiaries of North Bihar had received employment through doing extra works for some one whereas the corresponding figure for Central Bihar and Jharkhand was 01 and 10. Only 16

TABLE 3A.4

Selection of Works and Workers

Zone	*Selection of Works on the*				*Source of Information of JRY Works*						*Selection of Workers on the Recommendation of*						
	Gram Sabha	*Block office*	*NGO*	*Influ-ential person*	*BDO*	*VLW*	*Friends*	*NGO*	*Contr-actor*	*Any Other*	*Gram Sabha*	*VLW*	*BDO*	*NGO*	*Influ-ential person*	*Contr-actor*	*Any other*
North Bihar	44	06	00	10	00	00	19	00	41	00	00	00	00	00	00	59	01
Central Bihar	24	16	00	20	00	01	07	00	46	06	00	01	00	00	00	58	01
Jharkhand	50	05	00	05	00	02	24	00	33	01	00	01	00	00	12	45	02
Total	118	27	00	35	00	03	50	00	120	07	00	02	00	00	12	162	04

TABLE 3A.4A

Zone	*Selection of Works in the Felt needs of the People*		*Received Employment*				*Any Special Skill*	
	Yes	*No*	*By paying some money*	*By doing the work for some one*	*Proximity with the contractor*	*Any other*	*Yes*	*No*
North Bihar	59	01	01	35	16	08	10	50
Central Bihar	51	09	00	01	58	01	13	47
Jharkhand	53	07	00	10	46	04	17	43
Total	163	17	01	46	120	13	40	140

TABLE 3A.4B

Zone	*Work Available*		*Facilities Extended to Work Site*				
	Within the village	*Outside the village*	*Rest shelters*	*Drinking water*	*Creches*	*Others*	*No facility*
North Bihar	47	13	00	00	00	00	60
Central Bihar	42	18	08	05	00	00	47
Jharkhand	51	09	00	23	00	00	37
Total	140	40	08	28	00	00	144

(8.88%) beneficiaries of North Bihar had received works due to the proximity of the contractors whereas the corresponding figures for central Bihar and Jharkhand were 58 and 46 respectively. Hence overall impact of influential persons and contractors was apparent. 40 (22.2%) beneficiaries had some special skill whereas 140 (77.77%) beneficiaries were unskilled. (Table 3A.5). Works Different paragraph were available within the village in case of 140 (77.77%) beneficiaries whereas outside the village in case of 40 (22.22%) beneficiaries. 144 (80.0%) beneficiaries alleged that no facilities were extended to them during the work but 28 (15.55%) beneficiaries - 23 (82.14%) from Jharkhand and 5 (17.85%) from Central Bihar reported drinking water facilities, 8 (4.44%) beneficiaries of Central Bihar had received rest shelter during the work (Table 3A.6).

Works were executed by the contractors in case of all the 180 beneficiaries. Works were executed in the areas like inhabited predominantly by SCs/STs in case of 32 (17.77%) beneficiaries, concealed bonded labour in case of 3 (1.66%) beneficiaries, low wage pocket area in case of 108 (60.0%) beneficiaries, and randomly selected in case of 37 (20.55%) beneficiaries. (Table 3A.7).

54 (30.0%) beneficiaries reported that wage rate under JRY was higher than local wage rate. But 83 (46.11%) reported that wage rate was at par with the local wage rate. 43 (23.88%) beneficiaries reported that the wage rate was below the local wage rate. 77 (42.77%) beneficiaries had justified their participation in JRY, even if the wages were not higher than the local wage rate on the ground of availability of JRY work in lean agricultural season/non-availability of alternative employment. 45 (25.0%) had justified on the ground of JRY works close to their homesites. Only 4 (2.22%) had participated in the JRY work due to the easy work. Only 29 (16.11%) beneficiaries had awareness about minimum wage level whereas 151 (83.88%) had no awareness. Only 2 (1.11%) beneficiaries had accepted that the wages were paid to them in accordance to minimum wage act whereas 25 (13.75%) alleged that wages were not paid in accordance to the minimum wage act. 153 (85.0%) beneficiaries had no knowledge about the minimum wage level, so they were not in a position to give any opinion (Table 3A.8).

85 (47.22%) beneficiaries reported that there was

TABLE 3A.5

Execution of Works

Zone	Works Executed by					Works Executed in Area			
	Contractors	PRI's	Department	NGO	Any other	Inhabited predominantly by SC/ST	Concealed bounded labour	Low wage pocket area	Randomly selected
North Bihar	60	00	00	00	00	02	03	53	02
Central Bihar	60	00	00	00	00	20	00	24	16
Jharkhand	60	00	00	00	00	10	00	31	19
Total	180	00	00	00	00	32	03	108	37

TABLE 3A.6

Details about Wage

Zone	*Wage Rate*			*Awareness about Minimum Wage*		*Minimum Wage Rate is Paid*			*Reason to Work in Scheme if Wages are not Higher than Local Wage Rate*			
	At par with local rate	*Below local rate*	*Higher than local rate*	*Yes*	*No*	*Yes*	*No*	*No knowl-edge*	*Easy work*	*Available in lean agricultural season/Non-availability of work*	*Closer to home*	*Any other*
North Bihar	10	34	16	02	58	02	00	58	02	30	12	00
Central Bihar	20	08	32	10	50	00	10	50	00	22	06	00
Jharkhand	53	01	06	17	43	00	15	45	02	25	27	00
Total	83	43	54	29	151	02	25	153	04	77	45	00

TABLE 3A.6A

Zone	*Difference between the Wages of:*				*Mode of Payment of Wage*					*System of Payment of Wages*	
	Men/Women		*Skilled Unskilled*		*Daily*	*Weekly*	*Fortnightly*	*Monthly*	*No fixed period*	*Time bias*	*Piece, rated*
	Yes	*No*	*Yes*	*No*							
North Bihar	00	60	47	13	60	00	00	00	00	60	00
Central Bihar	25	35	55	05	08	25	00	00	27	44	16
Jharkhand	60	00	14	46	17	16	00	00	27	60	00
Total	85	95	116	64	85	41	00	00	54	164	16

TABLE 3A.7

Employment Generated

Zone	*Involvement of Workers in Different Works under the Scheme*				*Beneficiary or his Family get Benefitted in other Rural Development Programme*		*Name of Scheme which Benefitted the Beneficiary and or his Family*		
	One	*Two*	*Three*	*More*	*Yes*	*No*	*IRDP*	*EAS*	*Any other*
North Bihar	14	29	13	04	17	43	03	14	00
Central Bihar	08	24	17	11	11	49	11	00	00
Jharkhand	10	17	28	05	28	32	12	16	00
Total	32	70	58	20	56	124	26	30	00

TABLE 3A.8

No. of Days Worked

Zone	*No. of Days Worked*								*Actual number of days worked (average)*
	Less than 10 days	*11-15*	*16-20*	*21-30*	*31-40*	*41-60*	*61-80*	*81+*	
North Bihar	13	15	12	16	02	02	00	00	18.8
Central Bihar	04	06	06	12	07	15	09	01	38.5
Jharkhand	01	06	08	19	11	12	03	00	32.2
Total	18	27	26	47	20	29	12	01	29.8

difference of wages between men and women whereas 95 (52.77%) reported that there was no difference. But 116 (64.44%) beneficiaries reported that there was difference of wages between skilled and unskilled labourers whereas 64 (35.55%) reported that there was no difference. 85 (47.22%) reported that the mode of payment of wage was daily. 41 (22.77%) reported that it was weekly and 54 (30.0%) reported that there was no fixed period of payment of wage. 164 (91.11%) reported that the system of payment of wage was time -bias whereas only 16 (8.88%) beneficiaries of Central Bihar reported that the system of payment of wages was piece-rated (Table 3A.9).

32 (17.77%) beneficiaries had work in only one JRY scheme, 70 (38.88%) in two JRY schemes, 58 (32.2%) in three JRY schemes and 20 (11.11%) in four or more JRY schemes. 56 (31.11%) beneficiaries or their family members had been benefitted in other rural development programmes - 26 (46.24%) in IRDP and 30 (16.66%) in EAS. 124 (68.88%) beneficiaries or their family members had not taken the benefit of any rural development programme. (Table 3A.10)

18 (10.0%) beneficiaries had work less than 10 days under the JRY scheme, 27 (15.0%) in between 11-15 days, 26 (14.44%) in between 16-20 days, 47 (26.11%) in between 21-30 days, 20 (11.11%) in between 31-40 days, 29 (16.11%) in between 41-60 days, 12 (6.66%) in between 41-80 days and only 01 (0.55%) above 81 days. JRY had provided only 18.8 Mandays for the beneficiaries of North-Bihar, whereas the corresponding figures for Central Bihar and Jharkhand were 38.5 Mandays and 32.2 Mandays. (Table 3A.11).

156 (86.66%) beneficiaries reported that assets generated through the JRY were of durable nature, whereas 24 (13.33%) beneficiaries reported assets were of non-durable nature. 158 (87.77%) beneficiaries termed the expenditure of JRY as useful where 22 (12.22%) termed it wasteful. Out of 158 beneficiaries who termed it useful, 119 (75.31%) had termed it useful for the community as a whole, 30 (18.98%) had termed it useful for the weaker sections, 3 (1.66%) of Jharkhand had termed it useful only for the better-off section of society and 6 (3.22%) of the same region had termed it useful only for the vested interests. 115 (63.88%) beneficiaries opined that JRY assets had improved the production potential in the area, whereas 65 (36.11%) had

TABLE 3A.9

Assets Generated

Zone	*Nature of Assets*				*Useful to Whom*				*Have the Assets Improved the Production Potential*	
	Durable	*Non-durable*	*Useful*	*Wasteful*	*Community as a whole*	*Weaker section*	*Better-off section*	*Vested interest*	*Yes*	*No*
North Bihar	58	02	47	13	46	01	00	00	47	13
Central Bihar	55	05	58	02	44	14	00	00	58	02
Jharkhand	43	17	53	07	29	15	03	06	10	50
Total	156	24	158	22	119	30	03	06	115	65

TABLE 3A.9A

Zone	Work on School Building			Creation of Panchayat Ghar led to								
	Improved Enrolment of children in the school	Reduced drop-out	Improved educational standard	No impact	No work has been done for school building under JRY	More interaction and communication among people (social and political)	Greater awareness amongst people	Greater health care, hygiene etc.	No use due to Distance	No use due to Location	No use due to Other	Resource wastefulness
North Bihar	00	12	04	28	16	05	23	00	11	02	01	18
Central Bihar	01	00	05	00	54	00	05	00	19	36	00	00
Jharkhand	04	00	01	03	52	00	00	00	21	07	20	12
Total	05	12	10	31	122	05	28	00	51	45	21	30

TABLE 3A.10

General Awareness about Programme

Zone	*Has JRY Improved the Income of the Beneficiary*			*Have it led to Improvement in*					*Beneficiary's Observation*							*Investigator's Observation (Common for all the zone)*
	Marginal	*Significant*	*Moderate*	*Nutritional needs*	*Education of child*	*Social function*	*Savings*	*Clothing*	*Better house*	*Maintaining house hold consumption expenditure*	*Any other*	*Work should be done by the government or any other social agency not by contractor*	*Information should be given above minimum wages*	*Any other*	*No response*	
North Bihar	04	05	51	00	05	17	08	02	06	22	00	25	22	10	03	1. Contractors are compelled to pay 30%"of the sanctioned amount as speed money to the concerned authorities which results poor implementation.
Central Bihar	34	12	14	02	00	04	01	05	10	38	00	27	21	08	04	
Jharkhand	26	13	21	01	10	05	01	09	02	32	00	25	30	05	00	
Total	64	30	86	03	15	26	10	16	18	92	00	77	73	23	07	2. Mass awareness campaign needed about the programme and minimum wages.

3. Final payment to the contractor should be made after approval of a 'citizen committee' constituted to monitor the scheme.

opined that the assets generated through JRY had created no impact on the production potential in the area. (Table 3A.12).

Only 58 (32.22%) beneficiaries reported that school-building activity had been taken in their areas. 5 (2.77%) amongst them reported that better school conditions had improved the enrolment in the school. 12 (6.66%) from North Bihar reported that it had reduced the drop-out ratio and 10 (5.5%) claimed that it had improved the educational standard but 31 (17.22%) beneficiaries reported that there was no impact of the expenditure on school-building under JRY. 122 (67.77%) beneficiaries reported that no work had been done for school building under the JRY in their areas.

Only 5 (8.33%) beneficiaries in North Bihar had opined that the creation of Panchayat Ghar under JRY had led to more interaction and communication among people. 28 (46.66%) beneficiaries - 23 (82.14%) from North Bihar and 5 (17.85%) from South Bihar had opined that it had led to greater awareness among people, but 117 (65.0%) had opined that the creation of Panchayat Ghar had led to no use. 51 (28.33%) termed it unuseful due to distance factor, 45 (25.0%) due to location factor, 21 (11.66%) due to other reasons. 30 (16.66%) beneficiaries - 18 (60.0%) from North Bihar and 12 (40.0%) from Jharkhand termed creation of Panchayat Ghar as resource wastefulness. Hence, out of 60 beneficiaries of Jharkhand 48 (80.0%) termed it for no use and remaining 12 (20.0%) termed it complete resource wastefulness. (Table 3A.13).

(c) General Observations and Recommendations

All the 180 beneficiaries opined that the programme was quite useful. 64 (35.55%) beneficiaries reported that the programme had improved their income but marginally. 86 (47.77%) reported moderate improvement and 30 (16.66%) reported significant improvement in their income. 3 (1.66%) beneficiaries under JRY reported that their income had led to improvement in nutritional needs, 15 (8.33%) reported that their income had led to improvement in education of child, 26 (14.44%) in social function, 10 (5.55%) in savings, 16 (8.88%) in clothing, 18 (10.0%) in better housing, 92 (51.11%) in maintaining household consumption expenditure etc. 77 (42.77%) beneficiaries suggested that work should be done by the Government or any other social agencies not by the contractors. They complained about their exploitation by the contractors. 73 (40.55%) beneficiaries had suggested that there must be a wide publicity about the minimum wage level provided under the act. 23 (12.77%) had given different suggestion whereas 7 (3.88%) had given no response.

Investigators of all the three zones had gathered the information that the entire works under JRY had been done through the contractors. Contractors were compelled to pay 30% of the sanctioned amount as speed money to the concerned authorities which had resulted the poor implementation of the scheme. The investigators had given the following recommendations :

(i) effective steps should be given to curb the speed money amount,

(ii) mass awareness campaign was essential for the programme and the present level of minimum wages under the act.

(iii) final payment to the contractors should be made after the approval of citizens' committee constituted to monitor the scheme.

(d) Calculation of Poverty Indices

Head-Count ratio (H)

$$H = \frac{q}{n},$$

where q = No. of beneficiaries below poverty line
n = Total no. of beneficiaries

$$= \frac{147}{180}$$

$$= 0.82$$

Income-Gap ratio (I),

$$I = \frac{g}{\pi . q}, \quad \text{where } g = \sum_{i=1}^{n} gi$$

where g = p - yi

$$= \frac{1001100}{147 \times 21000}$$

p = Poverty line Income,

Yi = Income of i-th beneficiaries.

= 0.3242954

= 0.32

Ginni Co-efficient (G)

$$G = \frac{\text{Area of shaded region in fig.3A}}{0.5}$$

$$= \frac{0.13}{0.50} = 0.26$$

Now, Sen Index (P)

P= H {I + (1-I) G}

= 0.82 {0.32 + (1-0.32) x 0.26}

= 0.82 {0.32 + 0.68) x 0.26}

= 0.82 {0.32 + 0.18

= 0.82 x 0.50

= 0.41

B. EMPLOYMENT ASSURANCE SCHEME (EAS)

The scheme was launched on 2nd October, 1993 in 1775 identified backward blocks situated in drought prone, desert, tribal and hilly areas.

Subsequently, the scheme was extended to additional blocks including 722 blocks previously covered under the second stream of JRY. The scheme was universalised to cover all the rural blocks in the country w.e.f. 1.4.1997.

FIG. 3A

Income Inequality for JRY Beneficiaries

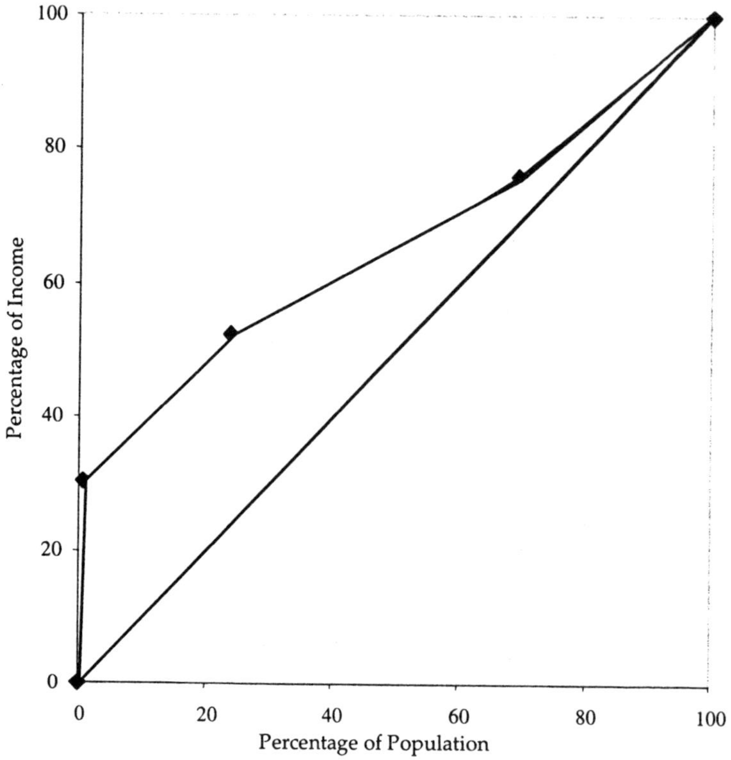

Percentage of Population	Percentage of Income
0	0
0.68	30.48
23.8	52.38
69.36	76.19
100	100

The main objective of the EAS is to provide about 100 days of assured casual manual employment during the lean agricultural season, at statutory minimum wages to all persons above the age of 18 years and below 60 years who need and seek employment on economically productive and labour intensive social and community works. The works are to be selected by the District collector and implemented through the line departments in such a manner that the ratio of wages to non-wage component would stand 60:40. A maximum of two adults per family are to be provided employment under the scheme.

The EAS is a centrally sponsored demand driven scheme under which no fixed allocations are made for the districts/ blocks. An initial national allocations are made to districts at the commencement of each year and thereafter depending on the demand for supplementary employment and the actual utilisation of funds, the districts can request for additional funds.

The study had evaluated the performance of the EAS to suggest viable measures for successful implementation of the scheme in future.

(a) Socio-economic Condition of the Beneficiaries

Out of 60 beneficiaries, 58 (96.66%) were male and only 02 (3.33%) were female. 100% beneficiaries of North Bihar and Jharkhand were male and the 2 female beneficiaries belonged to Central Bihar. It showed the least participation of women in the scheme.

38.33% beneficiaries were literate whereas 61.66% were illiterate. Out of 38.33% literate population, 33.33% had education below matriculation level and only 5.0% had the qualification of matriculation and above but below graduation level. Illiteracy level was higher in North Bihar, where 95.0% beneficiaries were illiterate and the only (5.0%) beneficiary had only primary education i.e., below matriculation level. Jharkhand was better placed. Out of 60 beneficiaries, 8.33% were farmers and 63.33% were agricultural labourers, 23.33% were non-agricultural casual labourers, and only 5.0% were non-agricultural self-employed. Agricultural labourers had taken maximum benefit of the scheme in North Bihar, Central

Bihar where the proportion was 100% and 70.0% respectively. Non-agricultural casual labourers had taken the benefits of the scheme in Jharkhand region where the proportion was 60.0% of the total beneficiaries of the region. (Table 3B.1)

46.66% had the family size of 1-5 persons, 53.33% had the family size of 6-11 persons and no beneficiary had the family size of 12 or more. 48.13% beneficiaries belonged to scheduled castes where only 3.33% belonged to scheduled tribes and 46.66% belonged to OBCs. Only a single beneficiary belonged to others category. Only 5.0% beneficiaries belonged to Ex/freed bonded labour and no one was the assignee of surplus land and remaining 95.0% beneficiaries belonged to others category. (Table - 3B.2)

No beneficiary in all the regions had income below Rs. 6401, 9 (15.0%) beneficiaries had income in between Rs 6401-11000, 29 (48.33%) beneficiaries had income in between Rs. 11001-16000 and 10 (16.66%) had income in between Rs. 16001-21000. Surprisingly, 10 (16.66%) beneficiaries had income in between Rs. 21001-32000 and only 2 (3.33%) had income above Rs. 32000. Hence, 12 (20.0%) beneficiaries did not come under the purview of the scheme on the basis of their income above poverty line. (Table 3B.3)

(b) Economic Structure and Viability of the Scheme

2 (3.33%) beneficiaries had received information about the scheme from the block development officer, 5 (8.33%) from V.L.W., 7 (11.66%) from friends, and 45 (75.0%) from contractors. Only 1 (1.66%) beneficiary had received information from other sources. 8 (13.33%) beneficiaries were selected for the works on the recommendations of the Gram Sabha and 4 (6.66%) on the recommendation of V.L.W., 3 (5.0%) on the recommendation of influential persons and 45 (75.0%) on the recommendation of the contractors. Hence the dominant role of contractors was well-established in the scheme as 100% beneficiaries of North Bihar and Central Bihar were selected by the contractors. But only 25.0% beneficiaries of the Jharkhand region were selected by the contractors and the remaining were selected by the Gram Sabha, V.L.W. and other influential persons. Jharkhand had shown the decentralized decision-making system on this score. (Table 3B.4)

TABLE 3B.1

Categorisation of Beneficiaries

Zone	Sex		Literacy		Literacy Level			Beneficiary's Occupation at the Time of Selection						
	Male	Female	Literate	Illiterate	Primary & above	Matric & above	Graduation & above	SF	MF	Agri-Labour	Non-agri. Casual Labour	Non-agri. Self employed	Artisan	Others
North Bihar	20	00	01	19	01	00	00	00	00	20	00	00	00	00
Central Bihar	18	02	08	12	05	03	00	01	00	14	02	03	00	00
Jharkhand	20	00	14	06	14	00	00	04	00	04	12	00	00	00
Total	58	02	23	37	20	03	00	05	00	38	14	03	00	00

TABLE 3B.2

Size of the Family and Social Classification

Zone	*Size of the Family*			*Social Classification*						
				Category I				*Category II*		
	1-5	*6-11*	*12+*	*SC*	*ST*	*OBCs*	*Others*	*Ex/freed bonded labour*	*Assignies of surplus land*	*Others*
North Bihar	07	13	00	14	00	05	01	00	00	20
Central Bihar	11	09	00	15	00	05	00	03	00	17
Jharkhand	10	10	00	00	02	18	00	00	00	20
Total	28	32	00	29	02	28	01	03	00	57

Table 3B.3

Family Income

Zone	*Below Poverty Line*			*Above Poverty Line*		
	Upto 6400	*6401-11000*	*11001-16000*	*16001-21000*	*21001-32000*	*32001+*
North Bihar	00	04	08	01	05	02
Central Bihar	00	03	10	04	03	00
Jharkhand	00	02	11	05	02	00
Total	00	09	29	10	10	02

49 (89.66%) beneficiaries had opined that the selections of the works were made on the felt need of the people. 20 (33.33%) had received work under the scheme by doing extra work for someone. 35 (58.33%) had received work due to proximity with the contractors and 5 (8.335) had received works through other sources. In brief, doing extra work for some influential persons and proximity with the contractors were the main sources for getting employment under the scheme. 16 (26.66%) beneficiaries had some special skill whereas 44 (73.33%) beneficiaries were unskilled. (Table 3B.4a)

Works were available within the villages in case of 34 (56.66%) beneficiaries whereas outside the village in case of 26 (43.33%) beneficiaries. 46 (76.66%) beneficiaries had alleged that no facility were extended to them during the work. 100% beneficiaries of North Bihar come under this category. Only 3 (15.0%) beneficiaries of Central Bihar had received drinking water facilities at the work site. Others had not received any facility. But 4 (20.0%) beneficiaries of Jharkhand region had received rest shelter facility at the work site and 7 (35.0%) of the region had received drinking water facility. Hence, treatment with the labourers was better at Jharkhand in comparison to North Bihar and Central Bihar. (Table 3B.4b)

Works under EAS were executed in the names of some Government employees at the block level but 100% beneficiaries had confirmed that the works were executed by the contractors in all the three survey zones. Works were executed in the areas like inhabited predominantly by SCs ad STs in case of 4 (6.66%)

TABLE 3B.4

Selection of Workers

Zone	*Source of Information of JRY Works*						*Selection of Workers on the Recommendation of*						
	BDO	*VLW*	*Friends*	*NGO*	*Contr-actor*	*Any Other*	*Gram Sabha*	*VLW*	*BDO*	*NGO*	*Influ-ential person*	*Contr-actor*	*Any other*
North Bihar	00	00	00	00	20	00	00	00	00	00	00	20	00
Central Bihar	00	00	03	00	16	01	00	00	00	00	00	20	00
Jharkhand	02	05	04	00	09	00	08	04	00	00	03	05	00
Total	02	05	07	00	45	01	08	04	00	00	03	45	00

TABLE 3B.4A

Zone	*Selection of Works in the Felt needs of the People*		*Received Employment*				*Any Special Skill*	
	Yes	*No*	*By paying some money*	*By doing the work for some one*	*Proximity with the contractor*	*Any other*	*Yes*	*No*
North Bihar	20	00	00	17	03	00	05	15
Central Bihar	15	05	00	00	20	00	03	17
Jharkhand	14	06	00	03	12	05	08	12
Total	49	11	00	20	35	05	16	44

TABLE 3B.4B

Zone	*Work Available*		*Facilities Extended to Work Site*				
	Within the village	*Outside the village*	*Rest shelters*	*Drinking water*	*Creches*	*Others*	*No facility*
North Bihar	05	15	00	00	00	00	20
Central Bihar	15	05	00	03	00	00	17
Jharkhand	14	06	04	07	00	00	09
Total	34	26	04	10	00	00	46

beneficiaries, low wage pocket area in case of 37 (61.66%) beneficiaries and randomly selected in case of 19 (31.66%) beneficiaries. (Table 3B.5)

36 (60.0%) beneficiaries reported that the wage rate under EAS was higher than the local wage rate. 21 (35.0%) beneficiaries reported that wage rate was at par with the local wage rate and only 3 (5.0%) reported that the wage rate was below the local wage rate. 4 (6.66%) beneficiaries justified their participation in EAS even if the wages were not higher than the local wage rate on the ground of availability of work in lean agricultural season/non-availability of alternative employment. 6 (10.0%) had justified their participation in the EAS due to easy nature of work, 12 (20.0%) had justified on the ground of EAS work close to their home sites. And only 2 (3.33%) had given other reasons. Only 14 (23.33%) beneficiaries had awareness about minimum wage level whereas 46 (76.66%) had no awareness. Only 2 (3.33%) beneficiaries had accepted that the wages were paid in accordance with the minimum wage level. 13 (24.66%) had alleged that wages were not paid in accordance with the minimum wage level. 45 (75.0%) had no knowledge about the minimum wage level. So they were not in a position to give any opinion. (Table 3B.6)

27 (45.0%) beneficiaries reported that there was difference of wages between men and women whereas 33 (55.0%) reported that there was no difference. 50% beneficiaries reported that there was difference of wage between skilled and unskilled labourers whereas other 50.0% beneficiaries had the opinion of no difference. Under the scheme. 34 (56.66%) reported that the mode of payment of wage was daily, 17 (28.33%) reported that it was weekly, and 9 (15.0%) reported that there was no fixed period of payment of wage. 53 (88.33%) reported that the system of payment of wages was time-bias whereas 07 (11.66%) beneficiaries only of North Bihar reported that the system of payment of wages was piece-rated. (Table 3B.6a)

22 (36.66%) beneficiaries had work in one EAS, 21 (35.0%) had work in two EAS, 11 (18.33%) in three EAS and only 06 (10.0%) in four or more EAS. 35 (58.33%) beneficiaries or their family members had been benefitted in other rural development programme - 28 (80.0%) in JRY and 7 (20.0%) in IRDP. 25 (41.66%) beneficiaries or their family members did not take the

TABLE 3B.5

Execution of Works

Zone	Works Executed by					Works Executed in Area			
	Contractors	PRI's	Department	NGO	Any other	Inhabited predominantly by SC/ST	Concealed bounded labour	Low wage pocket area	Randomly selected
North Bihar	20	00	00	00	00	00	00	20	00
Central Bihar	20	00	00	00	00	04	00	06	10
Jharkhand	20	00	00	00	00	00	00	11	09
Total	60	00	00	00	00	04	00	37	19

TABLE 3B.6

Details about Wage

Zone	*Wage Rate*			*Awareness about Minimum Wage*		*Minimum Wage Rate is Paid*			*Reason to Work in Scheme if Wages are not Higher than Local Wage Rate*			
	At par with local rate	*Below local rate*	*Higher than local rate*	*Yes*	*No*	*Yes*	*No*	*No knowl-edge*	*Easy work*	*Available in lean agricultural season/Non-availability of work*	*Closer to home*	*Any other*
North Bihar	03	03	14	00	20	00	00	20	00	04	00	02
Central Bihar	03	00	17	04	16	02	02	16	00	00	03	00
Jharkhand	15	00	05	10	10	00	11	09	06	00	09	00
Total	21	03	36	14	46	02	13	45	06	04	12	02

TABLE 3 B.6A

Zone	*Difference between the Wages of:*				*Mode of Payment of Wage*					*System of Payment of Wages*	
	Men/Women		*Skilled Unskilled*		*Daily*	*Weekly*	*Fortnightly*	*Monthly*	*No fixed period*	*Time bias*	*Piece rated*
	Yes	*No*	*Yes*	*No*							
North Bihar	00	20	09	11	13	07	00	00	00	13	07
Central Bihar	07	13	14	06	18	02	00	00	00	20	00
Jharkhand	20	00	07	13	03	08	00	00	09	20	00
Total	27	33	30	30	34	17	00	00	09	53	07

benefit of any rural development programme. (Table 3B.7)

8 (13.33%) beneficiaries had work less than 10 days under the EAS; 17 (28.33%) in between 11-15 days, 08 (13.33%) in between 16-20 days, 09 (15.0%) in between 21-30 days, 02 (3.33%) in between 31-40 days, 11 (18.33%) in between 41-60 days, and only 05 (8.33%) have above 61 days. EAS had provided 37.0 mandays for the beneficiaries of North Bihar, whereas the corresponding figures for Central Bihar and Jharkhand were only 13.1 mandays and 33.7 mandays. And the average mandays for the three sample zones was 27.93. Hence Central Bihar zone provided the least opportunity of work for the beneficiaries which was 13.1 only. (Table 3B.8)

53 (88.33%) beneficiaries reported that assets generated through the EAS were of durable nature, whereas only 07 (11.66%) beneficiaries reported that assets were of non-durable nature. 55 (91.66%) beneficiaries had termed the expenditure of EAS were useful whereas only 5 (8.33%) had termed it wasteful. Out of 55 beneficiaries who termed it useful, 41 (68.33%) had termed it useful for the community as a whole, 13 (21.66%) for the weaker sections, and only a single beneficiary from North Bihar had termed it useful for better-off section of society and not a single one had termed it useful for the vested interest. 47 (78.33%) beneficiaries opined that EAS assets had improved the production potential in the area whereas only 13 (21.66%) opined that the assets generated through EAS had created no impact on the production potential in the area. (Table 3B.9)

25.0% beneficiaries reported that the school-building activity had been taken up in their areas under the scheme. 1 (1.66%) beneficiary reported that work on school building had improved enrolment in that school. 6 (10.0%) reported that work on school building had reduced drop-out. 3 (5.0%) reported that betterment of school building had improved the educational standard whereas 5 (8.33%) opined that work on school building had created no impact. 45 (75.0%) beneficiaries reported that no work had been done on school building in their areas under the scheme. 22 (36.66%) beneficiaries had informed that no work had been done under EAS on Panchayat Ghar. All the 20 (100%) beneficiaries of Central Bihar came under this category. 6 (10.0%) beneficiaries, all from North Bihar had opined that Panchayat Ghar had led to better awareness among

Table 3B.7

Employment Generated

Zone	*Involvement of Workers in Different Works under the Scheme*				*Beneficiary or his Family get Benefitted in other Rural Development Programme*		*Name of Scheme which Benefitted the Beneficiary and or his Family*		
	One	*Two*	*Three*	*More*	*Yes*	*No*	*IRDP*	*EAS*	*Any other*
North Bihar	01	10	05	04	03	17	03	00	00
Central Bihar	16	04	00	00	18	02	15	03	00
Jharkhand	05	07	06	02	14	06	10	04	00
Total	22	21	11	06	35	25	28	07	00

TABLE 3B.8

No. of Days Worked

Zone	No. of Days Worked							Actual number of days worked (average)
	Less than 10 days	11-15	16-20	21-30	31-40	41-60	61+	
North Bihar	02	03	03	03	01	08	00	37.0
Central Bihar	04	12	03	01	00	00	00	13.1
Jharkhand	02	02	02	05	01	03	05	33.7
Total	08	17	08	09	02	11	05	27.9

TABLE 3B.9

Assets Generated

Zone	*Nature of Assets*				*Useful to Whom*				*Have the Assets Improved the Production Potential*	
	Durable	*Non-durable*	*Useful*	*Wasteful*	*Community as a whole*	*Weaker section*	*Better-off section*	*Vested interest*	*Yes*	*No*
North Bihar	20	00	15	05	11	03	01	00	19	01
Central Bihar	20	00	20	00	20	00	00	00	20	00
Jharkhand	13	07	20	00	10	10	00	00	08	12
Total	53	07	55	05	41	13	01	00	47	13

TABLE 3B.9A

Zone	Work on School Building					Creation of Panchayat Ghar led to							
	Improved Enrolment of children in the school	Reduced drop-out	Improved educational standard	No impact	No work has been done for school building under JRY	More interaction and communication among people (social and political)	Greater awareness amongst people	Greater health care, hygiene etc.	No use due to Distance	No use due to Location	Other	Resource wastefulness	No work has been done for Panchayat Ghar under EAS
North Bihar	01	06	02	02	09	00	06	02	02	01	00	09	00
Central Bihar	00	00	01	00	19	00	00	00	00	00	00	00	20
Jharkhand	00	00	00	03	17	00	00	00	05	01	02	11	02
Total	01	06	03	05	45	00	06	02	07	02	02	20	22

people. 2 (3.33%) both from North Bihar opined that it has led to greater health care/hygiene. 11 (18.33%) beneficiaries had termed it of no use. 7 (11.66%) termed it unuseful due to distance factor. 2 (3.33%) due to location factor and 2 (3.33%) due to other reasons. 19 (31.66%) beneficiaries 9 (47.36%) from North Bihar and 10 (52.63%) from Jharkhand termed it resource wastefulness. In brief, all the beneficiaries of Jharkhand region termed the expenditure on the Panchayat Ghar under the scheme either of no use or resource wastefulness. (Table 3B.10)

(c) General Observations and Recommendations

100% beneficiaries opined that the programme was useful but 26 (43.33%) reported that the programme had improed their programme marginally. 23 (38.33%) reported moderate improvement and 11 (18.33%) reported significant improvement in their income.

1 (1.66%) beneficiary had reported that his income had led to improvement in nutritional needs of his family. 112 (20.0%) reported that their income had led to improvement in education of child; 6 (10.0%) in social functions, 3 (5.0%) in savings, 3 (5.0%) in clothing, 6 (10.0%) in better housing and 29 (48.33%) in maintaining household consumption expenditure.

Beneficiary's Observations/Suggestions

Beneficiaries bserved that adequate level of employment couldn't be provided to them. Hence the scheme had shown a very little impact from employment generation points of view. They had alleged that they did not have proper information about the minimum wage level. That's why they had been exploited by the contractors.

Investigator's Observations/Recommendations

The investigators of all the three zones had given the following observations :

1. Selection of works under the scheme were based on lobby effect, not on the basis of priority.
2. Rate of speed money was higher in EAS in comparison to JRY, i.e, more than 30% of the Sanctioned amount as it was approved at district

TABLE 3B.10

General Awareness about Programme

Zone	Has JRY Improved the Income of the Beneficiary			Have it led to Improvement in								Beneficiary's Observation	Investigator's Observation (Common for all the zone)
	Marginal	*Significant*	*Moderate*	*Nutritional needs*	*Education of child*	*Social function*	*Savings*	*Clothing*	*Better house*	*Maintaining house hold consumption expenditure*	*Any other*		
North Bihar	00	03	17	00	08	02	02	01	03	04	00	1. Adequate level of employment could not be provided	1. Selection of works under the scheme are based on lobby effect, not on priorities
Central Bihar	20	00	00	01	00	00	01	01	01	16	00	2. Information should be given about minimum wages	2. Rate of speed money is higher in EAS in comaprison to JRY i.e. more than 30% of the sanctioned amount as it is approved at district level. Even the elected representatives take

												speed money for reommendation/selection of work.
Jharkhand	06	08	06	00	04	04	00	01	02	09	00	3. In addition to speed money contractors try to save at least 20% of the amount and the actual expenditure comes to less than 50% which results poor implementation and not according to estimate
Total	26	11	23	01	12	06	03	03	06	29	00	4. Work should be done through NGO's or people's cooperative.

level. Even the elected representatives had taken speed money for recommendation/selection of all.

3. Execution of the work had to be done in the name of block employees but in actual practice, the contractors execute the works.
4. In addition to speed money contractors tried to save 20% of the sanctioned amount and the actual expenditure on the scheme came to less than 50% which resulted poor implementation and not according to estimate.
5. For better performance works should be done through NGOs or Peoples' cooperatives.

(d) Calculation of Poverty Indices :

Head-Count ratio (H)

$$H = \frac{q}{n} = \frac{48}{60} = 0.80$$

$$I = \frac{g}{\pi . q} = \frac{351300}{21000 \times 48} = 0.3485119 = 0.35$$

Ginni Co-efficient

$G = 0.15$

Sen Index (P)

$$P = H \{I + (1-I) G\}$$

$$= 0.80 \{0.35 + (1-0.35) \times 0.15\}$$

$$= 0.80 \{0.35 + 0.65 \times 0.15\}$$

$$= 0.80 \{0.35 + 0.09\}$$

$$= 0.80 \times 0.44$$

$$= 0.342$$

An Analysis of Povety Index for the Scheme

The calculation of head-count ratio (H) shows that 80% of the beneficiaries were below poverty line. The calculation of income-gap ratio (I) gives a figure of 0.35. The value indicates

FIG. 3B

Income Inequality for EAS Beneficiaries

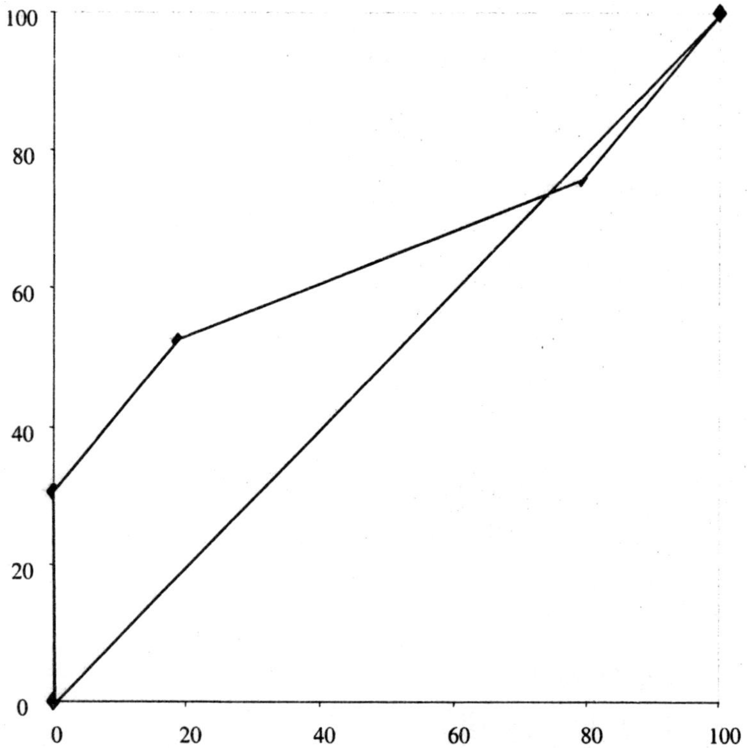

Percentage of Population	Percentage of Income
0	0
0	30.48
18.75	52.38
79.16	76.19
100	100

that the majority of the beneficiaries were in the upper income-slab below poverty line.

The value of Ginni co-efficient (G) is 0.15. In the calculation of G, the number of beneficiaries in the income group Rs. 11000-16000 is so large that the Lorenz curve even crosses the line of equality. This fact reduces the value of G. The lower value of G shows low degree of income disparity among the beneficiaries below poverty line.

The value of Sen-Index (0.34) symbolised that a large number of beneficiaries were in the upper income-slab below poverty line i.e., benefits are skewed in favour of upper-income group below poverty line.

CHAPTER

4

NATIONAL HOUSING SCHEME

A. INDIRA AWAAS YOJANA (IAY)

The IAY is the most important rural housing scheme which aims at providing dwelling units free of cost to the rural poor living below poverty line. IAY was part of JRY. But after restructuring of JRY, IAY became an independent centrally sponsored scheme for shelter for rural poor with resources being shared on a 80:20 ratio between centre and states. The main objective of the scheme is to construct dwelling units free of cost for the target group below the poverty line which comprises SC/ST, freed bonded labourers and also non SC/ST families. The cost norms under IAY have been periodically increased as per the Ninth Five Year Plan document, the maximum ceiling of assistance admissible under IAY has been raised from Rs. 14000 to Rs. 20000 in plain areas and Rs. 15,800 to Rs. 22,000 in the hilly/difficult areas.

The IAY had a limited format of construction of new houses. But in the modified form IAY has two components;

(i) Construction of new houses (at an average weighted cost of Rs. 20,000)

(ii) Upgradation of katchha and unserviceable houses (at a unit cost Rs. 10000). States are allowed to use up to 20% of the funds allocated under IAY for the upgradation of unserviceable katchha houses.

The different dimensions of the scheme had been verified under the field survey.

(a) Socio-economic Condition of the Beneficiaries

Out of 60 beneficiaries 33 (55.0%) were male and 27 (45.0%) were female. 18 (30.0%) beneficiaries were literate and 42 (70.0%) were illiterate. Out of 18 literate beneficiaries 17 (94.44%) beneficiaries had the qualification of primary level and above but below matriculation level, only a single (5.55%) beneficiary hailing from Jharkhand had the qualification of matriculation level but below graduation level. Not a single beneficiary could reach upto graduation level. Illiteracy level was higher (45.23%) in Central Bihar being followed by North Bihar (only 38.09%).

Out of 60 beneficiaries, only 02 (5.0%) were small farmers, no one was there for marginal farming. But 31 (51.66%) were agricultural labourers, 11 (18.33%) were non-agricultural labourers, 11 (18.33%) were non-agricultural self employed, not a single beneficiary was artisan but 04 (6.66%) were others including housewives. Hence agricultural labourers had taken the maximum benefit from the scheme specially in Central Bihar where 95% beneficiaries were agricultural labourers. (Table 4A.1)

31.66% beneficiaries had the family size of 1-5 members, 68.33% had the size 6-11 members and no one had the family size of 12 or more. The trend was almost similar in all three zones.

31 (51.66%) beneficiaries belonged to scheduled caste, 3 (5.0%) belonged to scheduled Tribe (only form Jharkhand region), 20 (33.33%) belonged to OBCs and 6 (10.0%) from other castes group including minority. Only 3 (5.0%) beneficiaries were freed bonded labourers and 3 (5.0%) were assignies of surplus land from Central Bihar and Jharkhand region respectively. Remaining 54 (90.0%) belonged to other category. (Table 4A.2)

Only 1 (.66%) beneficiary belonged to Jharkhand region had income below Rs. 6401, 7 (11.66%) had income in between Rs. 6401-11000, 25 (41.66%) had income in between Rs. 11001-16000 and 13 (21.66%) had income in between Rs. 16001-21000, 14 (23.33%) beneficiaries had income in between Rs. 21001-

TABLE 4A.1

Categorisation of Beneficiaries

Zone	*Sex*		*Literacy*		*Literacy Level*			*Beneficiary's Occupation at the Time of Selection*						
	Male	*Female*	*Literate*	*Illiterate*	*Primary & above*	*Matric & above*	*Graduation & above*	*SF*	*MF*	*Agri-Labour*	*Non-agri. Casual Labour*	*Non-agri. Self employed*	*Artisan*	*Others*
North Bihar	16	04	04	16	04	00	00	00	00	09	06	04	00	01
Central Bihar	03	17	01	19	01	00	00	00	00	19	00	01	00	00
Jharkhand	14	06	13	07	12	01	00	03	00	03	05	06	00	03
Total	03	27	18	42	17	01	00	03	00	31	11	11	00	04

TABLE 4A.2

Size of the Family and Social Classification

Zone	*Size of the Family*			*Social Classification*						
				Category I				*Category II*		
	1-5	*6-11*	*12+*	*SC*	*ST*	*OBCs*	*Others*	*Ex/freed bonded labour*	*Assignies of surplus land*	*Others*
North Bihar	05	15	00	10	00	06	04	00	00	20
Central Bihar	06	14	00	20	00	00	00	03	00	17
Jharkhand	08	12	00	01	03	14	02	00	03	17
Total	19	41	00	31	03	20	06	03	03	54

32000. This group was above the poverty line but managed to take the benefit of the scheme with their manipulating skill including the payment of high speed money. (Table 4A.3)

(b) Economic Structure and Viability of the Scheme

100% beneficiaries had taken the benefit of the scheme for construction of housing. Under the scheme houses had to be constructed by the beneficiaries themselves. 50 (83.33%) beneficiaries had reported that they had constructed their houses themselves but 9 (45.0%) beneficiaries of North Bihar reported that their houses had been constructed by influential persons including bricks manufacturers, only (1.66%) a single respondent had reported that his house was constructed by the contractor. (Table 4A.4)

Only 20 (33.33%) beneficiaries were satisfied with the work. and remaining 40 (66.66%) were dissatisfied. 32 (80.0%) amongst them were not satisfied as the amount was not adequate. 8 (20.0%) were dissatisfied due to appropriation of a sizeable proportion of amount by the concerned authority. Not even a single beneficiary from Jharkhand region was satisfied. (4A.5)

53 (88.83%) respondent reported that they had paid for their inclusion in IAY scheme. Only 7 (11.66%) reported that they had not paid any amount for the purpose. 10 (16.66%) beneficiaries had paid below Rs. 501, 13 (21.66%) in between Rs. 501-1000, 18 (30.0%) in between Rs. 1001-1500, 11 (18.33%) in between Rs. 1501-2000, and only 1 (1.66%) of Central Bihar above Rs. 2001. He belonged to upper caste. 2 (3.77%) beneficiaries paid the speed money to the Panchayat authority (Gram Sevak). 31 (58.41%) paid to the concerned block authority and 20 (37.73) to the middlemen. The trend was almost similar in all the three zones. (Table 4A.6)

(c) General Observations and Recommendations

Only 18 (30.0%) had accepted that IAY help would raise their income level. 41 (70.0%) had opined that there would be no change in their income level due to IAY help. 10 (16.66%) beneficiaries had given this opinion on the ground that IAY house provided no major change in the living standard. 31 (51.66%) beneficiaries had given this opinion on the ground that

TABLE 4A.3

Family Income

Zone	*Below Poverty Line*			*Above Poverty Line*		
	Upto 6400	*6401-11000*	*11001-16000*	*16001-21000*	*21001-32000*	*32001+*
North Bihar	00	04	10	00	06	00
Central Bihar	00	01	06	10	03	00
Jharkhand	01	02	09	03	05	00
Total	01	07	25	13	14	00

TABLE 4A.4

Construction of Machinery

Zone	*Purpose*		*Construction through*				
	Repair-ing	*Construc-tion*	*Your-self*	*Contr-actor*	*Block authority*	*Panchayat authority*	*Any other*
North Bihar	00	20	11	00	00	00	09 (influential person)
Central Bihar	00	20	20	00	00	00	00
Jharkhand	00	20	19	01	00	00	00
Total	00	60	50	01	00	00	09

other conditions were the same and only 1 (1.66%) beneficiary had given other reason in favour of his argument.

Beneficiary's Observations

Beneficiaries of the scheme had given the following broad observations :

(i) The amount paid was inadequate.
(ii) Payment of speed money was more/less than essential condition to get the benefit of the scheme.
(iii) The rate of speed money was about 10% of the sanctioned amount.

TABLE 4A.5

Satisfaction Level

Zone	*Satisfied with Work*		*Not Satisfied as:*		
	Yes	*No*	*Amount not adequate*	*Appropriation of amount by concerned authorities*	*Any other*
North Bihar	17	03	03	00	00
Central Bihar	03	17	11	06	00
Jharkhand	00	20	18	02	00
Total	20	40	32	08	00

(iv) There was no provision for power supply to them at a subsidised rate.

(v) Persons above poverty line took benefit of the scheme through manipulations.

Investigators Observations and Recommendations

On the basis of cross-survey the investigators had confirmed that the amount should be raised in proportion of decline in money value per annum.

In addition, the action should be taken in case of any complain regarding speed money.

(d) Calculation of Poverty Indices

Head-Count ratio :

$$H = \frac{q}{n} = \frac{47}{60} = 0.783$$

Income-gap ratio :

$$I = \frac{g}{\pi . q} = \frac{335400}{21000x47} = 0.3398176$$

Ginni Co-efficient :

TABLE 4A.6

Payment for Selection

Zone	Payment for Selection		Amount						Amount taken by		
	Yes	No	0	1-500	501-1000	1001-1500	1501-2000	2001+	Panchayat authority	Block authority	Middle-man
North Bihar	16	04	04	08	06	00	02	00	00	10	06
Central Bihar	19	01	01	00	05	05	08	01	00	13	06
Jharkhand	18	02	02	02	02	13	01	00	02	08	08
Total	53	07	07	10	13	18	11	01	02	31	20

TABLE 4A.7

Gains from IAY

Zone	*IAY help would Raise Income Level*		*IAY Help would not Raise Income as*			*Beneficiary's Observation*	*Investigator's Observation*
	Yes	*No*	*No Major change in living standard*	*Other conditions are the same*	*Any other*		
North Bihar	06	14	01	12	01	1. Inadequate amount	1. Amount should be raised in proportion of decline in money value per annum.
Central Bihar	06	14	04	10	00	2. Payment of speed money is more/less an essential condition to get the benefit of the scheme.	2. Harsh action should be taken in case of any complain of speed money.
Jharkhand	06	14	05	09	00	3. The rates of speed money is about 10% of the sanctioned amount.	
Total	18	42	10	31	01	4. Subsidised power supply should be made to them. 5. Persons above poverty line take benefit of the scheme through manipulations.	

FIG. 4A

Income Inequality for IAY Beneficiaries

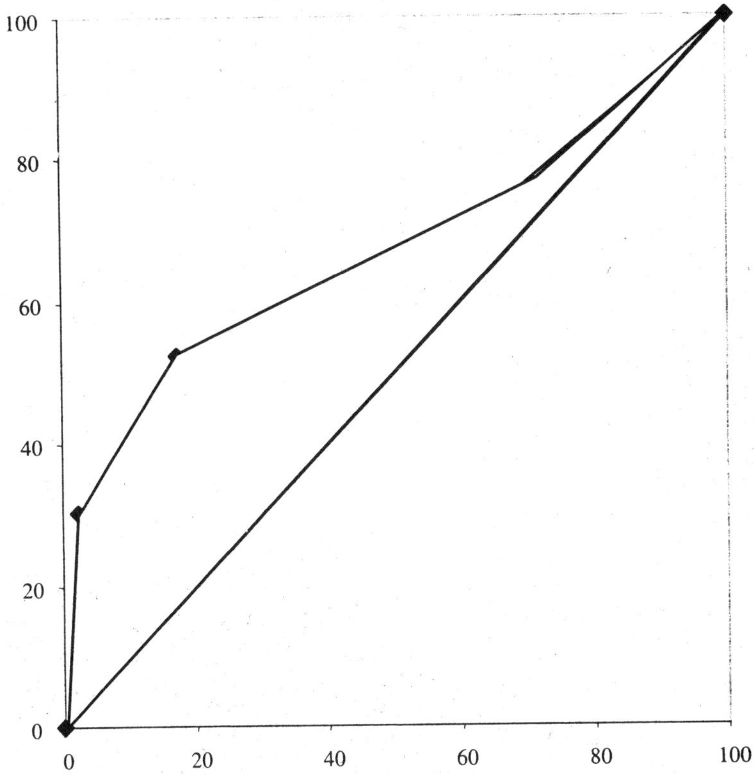

Percentage of Population	Percentage of Income
0	0
2.17	30.48
17.34	52.38
71.73	76.19
100	100

$G = 0.16$

Sen Index (P)

$P = .H \{I + (1\text{-}I)\ G\}$

$= 0.78\ [0.34 + (1\text{-}0.34)\ 0.16]$

$= 0.78\ [0.34 + 0.66 \times 0.16]$

$= 0.78\ [0.34 + 0.10]$

$= 0.78 \times 0.44$

$= 0.34$

An Analysis of Poverty Index for the Scheme

The calculation of Head-Count Ratio (H) shows that 78% the beneficiaries are below poverty line. The estimated value of Income gap ratio (I) gives a figure of 0.34. The value indicates that the majority of the beneficiaries are in the upper income slab below poverty line.

The value of Ginni co-efficient (G) is 0.16 which shows a very low degree of income disparity among the beneficiaries below the poverty line.

The computed Sen index, 0.34, indicates that a large number of beneficiaries were in the upper income slab below poverty line. In this case the value of Sen index and the Income gap ratio gives the same result numerically.

CHAPTER

5

NATIONAL SOCIAL ASSISTANCE PROGRAMME (NSAP)

The NSAP came into effect from 15th August 1995 as a significant step towards the fulfilment of Directive Principles in Article 41 and 42 of the constitution through the enunciation of a National Policy for social assistance benefits to poor households living below the poverty line in case of old age, death of primary breadwinner and maternity. It is a centrally sponsored scheme with 100 per cent central assistance provided to states/UTs. The scheme is implemented in the states/UTs through Panchayats and Municipalities.

A. National Old Age Pension Scheme (NOAPS)
B. National Family Benefit Scheme (NFBS)
C. National Maternity Benefit Scheme (NMBS)

All the three components of the NSAP had been separately evaluated on the basis of field survey.

A. NATIONAL OLD AGE PENSION SCHEME (NOAPS)

Under NOAPS old age pension of Rs. 75 per month was provided to persons of 65 years and above who were destitutes. The scheme could be linked to medical care and other benefits aimed at the aged beneficiaries. The efficiency of the scheme had been evaluated under the micro level study.

(a) Socio-economic Condition of the Beneficiaries

Out of 60 beneficiaries, 17 (28.33%) were male and 43 (71.66%) were female. Only 12 (20.0%) beneficiaries were literate and 48 (80.0%) were illiterate. Out of 12 beneficiaries, all of them i.e., 100% beneficiaries had the qualification of Primary level. No beneficiary was there in all the zones who had qualified either the matriculation or graduation level. Illiteracy level was higher in North Bihar (90.0%) followed by Central Bihar (85.0%). Out of 60 beneficiaries, only 4 (6.66%) were small farmers, 3 (5.0%) were marginal farmers.

All the beneficiaries of both the categories hailed from Central Bihar. 15 (25.0%) were agricultural labourers and 05 (8.33%) hailing only from Jharkhand were non-agricultural labourers, 18 (30.0%) were non-agricultural self employed, Not a single one belonged to artisan group, but 15 (25.0%) were others including housewives. Hence, it was clear that non-agricultural labourers had taken the maximum benefit of the scheme. Agricultural labourers and others maintained the equality. (Table 5A.1)

41.66% beneficiaries had the family size of 1-5 members, 53.33% had the size of 6-11 members and only 5.0% had the size of 12 or more. Jharkhand was lacking the size of 12 or more. 15 (25.0%) beneficiaries belonged to scheduled caste, not a single beneficiary belonged to scheduled tribe group, 37 (61.66%) belonged to OBCs. and only 8 (13.33%) belonged to others groups including minority. And 3 (5.0%) beneficiaries hailed from only Central Bihar were freed bonded labourers, not a single one was there the assignee of surplus land but remaining 57 (95.0%) belonged to others category. (Table 5A.2)

Out of 60 beneficiaries, 8 (13.33%) had income below Rs. 6401 only 5 (8.33%) had income in between Rs. 6401-11000, 12 (20.0%) in between Rs. 11001-16000, 13 (21.66%) in between Rs. 16001-21000, 16 (26.66%) beneficiaries had income in between Rs. 21001-32000. 6 (10.0%) had income above Rs. 32000. Hence 22 (36.66%) beneficiaries had income above poverty line but they had managed to get the benefit of the scheme with their manipulating skill including payment of speed money (Table 5A.3).

TABLE 5A.1

Categorisation of Beneficiaries

Zone	Sex		Literacy		Literacy Level			Beneficiary's Occupation at the Time of Selection						
	Male	Female	Literate	Illiterate	Primary & above	Matric & above	Graduation & above	SF	MF	Agri-Labour	Non-agri. Casual Labour	Non-agri. Self employed	Artisan	Others
North Bihar	04	16	02	18	02	00	00	00	00	10	00	03	00	07
Central Bihar	05	15	03	17	03	00	00	04	03	04	00	06	00	03
Jharkhand	08	12	07	13	07	00	00	00	00	01	05	09	00	05
Total	17	43	12	48	12	00	00	04	03	15	05	18	00	15

TABLE 5A.2

Size of the Family and Social Classification

Zone	*Size of the Family*			*Social Classification*						
				Category I				*Category II*		
	1-5	*6-11*	*12+*	*SC*	*ST*	*OBCs*	*Others*	*Ex/freed bonded labour*	*Assignies of surplus land*	*Others*
North Bihar	05	14	01	06	00	08	06	00	00	20
Central Bihar	11	07	02	07	00	12	01	03	00	17
Jharkhand	09	11	00	02	00	17	01	00	00	20
Total	25	32	03	15	00	37	08	03	00	57

TABLE 5A.3

Family Income

Zone	Below Poverty Line			Above Poverty Line		
	Upto 6400	6401-11000	11001-16000	16001-21000	21001-32000	32001+
North Bihar	01	03	02	05	09	00
Central Bihar	04	00	05	02	04	05
Jharkhand	03	02	05	06	03	01
Total	8	05	12	13	16	06

(b) Economic Structure and Viability of the Scheme

Amount of Rs. 75 per month had been fixed for the scheme or but the mode of payment was not regular. 100% beneficiaries reported that there had been no fixed time frame for them to receive the amount. Out of 60 beneficiaries only 21 (35.0%) had received the amount in full whereas 39 (65.0%) beneficiaries had not received the amount in full. (Table 5A.4)

38 (63.33%) beneficiaries had paid the speed money for inclusion in pensioners list. Only 22 (36.66%) reported that they did not pay any speed money for the purpose. Out of 38 beneficiaries only 5 (13.15%) had paid the amount below Rs. 51, 14 (36.84%) had paid the amount in between Rs. 51-100, 6 (15.78%) in between Rs. 101-150, 5 (13.15%) in between Rs. 151-200, and 8 (21.05%) had paid the amount above Rs. 200. Out of 38 beneficiaries , 16 (42.10%) beneficiaries reported that the speed money had been appropriated by the concerned block authority, only a single (2.63%) beneficiary had reported that the speed money had been appropriated Panchayat authority and 21 (55.26%) by the middleman. (Table 5A.5)

(c) General Observation and Recommendation

Out of 60, 25 (41.66%) beneficiaries used the amount for own purpose but 35 (58.33%) beneficiaries had not used the amount for own purpose. Out of 35 beneficiaries, 31 (88.57%) reported they used the amount for family, only 2 (5.71%) hailed only from North Bihar used the amount for loan repayment and remaining 2 (5.71%) only hailed from Central Bihar used the

TABLE 5A.4

Process of Assistance

Zone	*Mode of Payment*						*Received Amount in Full*	
	Amount (per month)	*Monthly*	*Quarterly*	*Half yearly*	*Yearly*	*No fixed period*	*Yes*	*No*
North Bihar	75	00	00	00	00	20	18	02
Central Bihar	75	00	00	00	00	20	03	17
Jharkhand	75	00	00	00	00	20	00	20
Total	225	00	00	00	00	60	21	39

Table 5A.5

Speed Money for the Scheme

Zone	*Paid Speed Money for Inclusion in Pensioners List*		*Amount of Speed Money*						*Speed Money taken by:*		
	Yes	*No*	*0*	*1-50*	*51-100*	*101-150*	*151-200*	*200+*	*Block authority*	*Panchayat authority*	*Middle-man*
North Bihar	08	12	12	03	04	01	00	00	07	00	01
Central Bihar	14	06	06	01	02	01	02	08	06	00	08
Jharkhand	16	04	04	01	08	04	03	00	03	01	12
Total	38	22	22	05	14	06	05	08	16	01	21

TABLE 5A.6

Use of the Assistance and General Observations

Zone	*Beneficiary Uses the Amount for Own Purpose*		*Beneficiary Uses the Amount for*			*Assistance Amount has Significance for the Beneficiay*		*Beneficiary's Observation*	*Investigator's Observation*
	Yes	*No*	*Family*	*Loan repay-ment*	*Other purposes*	*Yes*	*No*		
North Bihar	05	15	13	02	00	08	12	Payment should be made regularly through account transfer system of a bank or post office	1. A sizeable proportion of beneficiaries have income above poverty line.
Central Bihar	12	08	06	00	02	14	06		2. Few beneficiaries have age much below 65 years
Jharkhand	08	12	12	00	00	18	02		Suggestions : 1. A definite age and income proof should be needed for beneficiaries selection.
Total	25	35	31	02	02	40	20		2. Payment should be made through account transfer on monthly basis 3. Harsh action should be taken in case of any genuine complain.

amount for other purposes. 40 (66.66%) beneficiaries reported that the assistance amount had significance for them. But the remaining 20 (33.33%) reported that the assistance amount had no significance for them.

Beneficiary's Observations

Beneficiaries of the scheme observed that the main weakness of the scheme was that there was no time frame for the payment of the amount. They suggested that the payment should be made regularly i.e., monthly basis through account transfer system of a bank or post office.

Investigators Observations and Recommendations

On the basis of cross-survey the investigators confirmed that:

(i) a sizeable proportion of beneficiaries had income above poverty line.
(ii) few beneficiaries had age much below 65 years.

Recommendations

(i) A definite age and income proof should be needed for beneficiaries selection.
(ii) Payment should be made through account transfer on monthly basis at the nearest bank or post office.
(iii) Harsh action should be taken in case of any genuine complain.

(d) Calculation of Poverty Indices

Head-Count ratio :

$$H = \frac{q}{n} = \frac{37}{60} = 0.6166$$

Income-gap ratio :

$$I = \frac{g}{\pi . q} = \frac{298200}{21000 x 37} = 0.3837$$

FIG. 5A

Income Inequality for NOAPS Beneficiaries

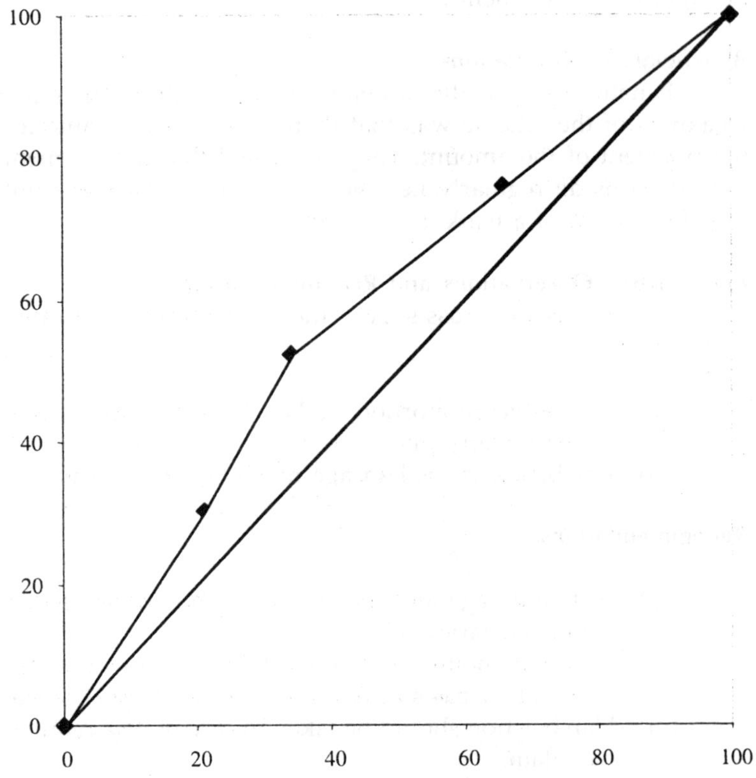

Percentage of Population	Percentage of Income
0	0
21.05	30.48
34.21	52.38
65.78	76.19
100	100

Ginni Co-efficient :

G = 0.15

Sen-Index (P)

P = H {I + (1-I) G}

= 0.62 [0.38 + (1-0.38) 0.09]

= 0.62 [0.38 + 0.62 x 0.09]

= 0.62 [0.38 + 0.06]

= 0.62 x 0.44

= 0.27

An Analysis of Poverty Index for the Scheme

The Head-Count Ratio value for the scheme shows that approximately 62% of the beneficiaries were below poverty line. The Income-gap ratio viz 0.38 reveals that most of the beneficiaries were in the upper-income group below poverty line.

The calculated value of Ginni co-efficient (G) is 0.09 which designates a very-very low degree of income disparity among the beneficiaries.

The value of Sen-index (0.27) shows that a very large number of beneficiaries were in the upper-income slab below poverty line. With a very low value of G, the Sen-index gives a large value. This is due to the fact that Head-Count Ratio and Income gap ratio are having larger valued.

B. NATIONAL FAMILY BENEFIT SCHEME (NFBS)

The NFBS provides a lump sum family benefit of Rs. 10000 to the bereaved household in case of death of the primary bread winner irrespective of the cause of death. This scheme is applicable to all the eligible persons in the age group of 18-64. Attempt had been made to evaluate the efficiency of the scheme with the help of the field survey.

(a) Socio-economic Conditions of the Beneficiaries

Out of 32 beneficiaries, only 2 (6.25%) were male and 30

(93.75%) were female. Only 12 (37.5%) were literate and 20 (62.5%) were illiterate. Out of this 12 literate beneficiaries, 11 (91.66%) had the qualification of primary and above level but below matriculation level and only, a single (8.33%) beneficiary had the qualification of matriculation and above but below graduation level but not a single one could reach upto graduation level. Out of 32 beneficiaries only 2 (6.25%) were small farmers, not a single one was a marginal farmer. 5 (25.625%) hailed from North Bihar were agricultural labourers, and other 5 (125.625%) hailed from Jharkhand were non-agricultural casual labourers, 14 (43.75%) were non-agricultural self-employed, there was no one in the artisan group and only 6 (18.75%) were others including housewives. It was clear that the non-agricultural self-employed had taken the maximum benefit from the scheme. (Table 5B.1)

50.0% beneficiaries had the family size of 1-5 members, other 50.0% had the size of 6-11 members, but not a single one had the size of 12 or more 7 (21.875%) beneficiaries belonged to scheduled caste, only 1 (3.125%) belonged to scheduled tribe group, 18 (56.25%) belonged to OBCs and 6 (18.75%) belonged to others group including minority. Neither a single beneficiary was freed bonded labour, nor a assignee of surplus land. But 100% belonged to others category (Table 5B.2).

Out of 32 beneficiaries, only a single (3.125%) beneficiary who hails only from Jharkhand had income below Rs. 6401, 3 (9.375%) had in between Rs. 6401-11000, 20 (62.5%) in between Rs. 11001-16000, 7 (21.875%) in between Rs. 16001-21000, and only 1 (3.125%) hailing from North Bihar had income above poverty line. This beneficiary managed to get the benefit of the scheme with his manipulating skill including payment of speed money. (Table 5B.3)

(b) Economic Structure and Viability of the Scheme

Out of 32 beneficiaries, 30 (93.75%) beneficiaries were the wives of the deceased and only 2 (6.25) were sons of deceased.

28 (87.5%) beneficiaries reported that they had paid the speed money to the block authority whereas 4 (12.5%) of North Bihar reported that they had not paid it. No beneficiary was there who paid speed money below Rs. 101 to the concerned block authority. 3 (10.71%) paid in between Rs. 101-200, 8

TABLE 5B.1

Categorisation of Beneficiaries

Zone	Sex		Literacy		Literacy Level			Beneficiary's Occupation at the Time of Selection						
	Male	Female	Literate	Illiterate	Primary & above	Matric & above	Graduation & above	SF	MF	Agri-Labour	Non-agri. Casual Labour	Non-agri. Self employed	Artisan	Others
North Bihar	01	08	00	09	00	00	00	00	00	05	00	01	00	03 (House wife)
Central Bihar	00	03	00	03	00	00	00	02	00	00	00	01	00	00
Jharkhand	01	19	12	08	11	01	00	00	00	00	05	12	00	03 (House wife)
Total	02	30	12	20	11	01	00	02	00	05	05	14	00	06

TABLE 5B.2

Size of the Family and Social Classification

Zone	*Size of the Family*			*Social Classification*						
				Category I				*Category II*		
	1-5	*6-11*	*12+*	*SC*	*ST*	*OBCs*	*Others*	*Ex/freed bonded labour*	*Assignies of surplus land*	*Others*
North Bihar	05	04	00	03	00	02	04	00	00	09
Central Bihar	01	02	00	01	00	02	00	00	00	03
Jharkhand	10	10	00	03	01	14	02	00	00	20
Total	16	16	00	07	01	18	06	00	00	32

TABLE 5B.3

Family Income

Zone	*Below Poverty Line*			*Above Poverty Line*		
	Upto 6400	*6401-11000*	*11001-16000*	*16001-21000*	*21001-32000*	*32001+*
North Bihar	00	01	07	00	01	00
Central Bihar	00	00	01	02	00	00
Jharkhand	01	02	12	05	00	00
Total	01	03	20	07	01	00

(28.57%) paid in between Rs. 201-300, 4 (14.28%) paid in between Rs. 301-400, and 13 (46.42%) in between Rs. 401-500 but not a single one was there to pay above Rs. 500. 10 (31.25%) beneficiaries reported that they had paid the speed money to the concerned district authority. Only a single beneficiary hailing from North Bihar paid the speed money amount below Rs. 251 to the concerned district authority other of the same region had paid in between Rs. 251-500, 4 (12.5%) had paid in between Rs. 501-1000, other 4 (12.5%) had paid in between Rs. 1001-2000, while no one had paid above Rs. 2001.

Out of 32 beneficiaries, 20 (100.0%) beneficiaries of Jharkhand region paid speed money only at block level, 8 beneficiaries of North Bihar and Central Bihar paid speed money at both the places i.e., block level and district level but 2 beneficiaries of North Bihar paid speed money only at district level. Only 2 beneficiaries of North Bihar had not paid any amount of speed money either at block level or at district level. 9 beneficiaries paid directly to the office. 18 beneficiaries to the middle men and 3 to others including bank employees.

(c) General Observation and Recommendations

Out of 32 beneficiaries, 10 (31.25%) reported that they had utilised the amount of consumption expenditure, 8 (25.0%) had utilised to undertake productive activity, 11 (34.375%) had utilised to repay the loan, and remaining 3 (9.375%) hailing from only Central Bihar had utilised on other purposes. (Table 5B.5)

TABLE 5B.4

Process of Assistance

Zone	*Benefi-ciary's Relation with Decrease*		*Payment of Speed Money to Block Authority*		*Amount of Speed Money taken by Block Authority*							*Payment of Speed Money*		*Amount of Speed Money taken by District Authority*						*Who had taken the Amount*		
	Wife	*Son*	*Yes*	*No*	*0*	*1-100*	*101-200*	*201-300*	*301-400*	*401-500*	*501+*	*Yes*	*No*	*0*	*1-250*	*251-500*	*501-1000*	*1001-2000*	*2001+*	*Directly the Ofice*	*Middle-man*	*Others*
North Bihar	08	01	05	04	04	00	01	02	00	02	00	07	02	02	01	01	01	04	00	02	04	'01 (Bank)
Central Bihar	03	00	03	00	00	00	00	00	00	03	00	03	00	00	00	00	03	00	00	00	03	'00
Jharkhand	19	01	13	07	00	00	02	06	04	08	00	00	20	20	00	00	00	00	00	07	11	02
Total	30	02	21	11	04	00	03	08	04	13	00	10	22	22	01	01	04	04	00	09	18	'03

Beneficiaries Observations

Beneficiaries of the scheme had pointed out the following observations :

1. Procedural delay should be avoided by simplification of the process.
2. In case of death outside the local area, beneficiaries had to face a lot of problems in obtaining death certificate. This created a lot of problems specifically in case of migrant labour. Alternative should be evolved to save the beneficiaries from harassment on the score.

Investigators Observations and Recommendations

On the basis of cross-survey the Investigators confirmed that:

(i) Amount of speed money in the scheme was high as the Government pays Rs. 10000/- at a time.

(ii) The authorities created a number of obstacles in case of no payment or less payment of speed money.

Suggestions

1. The payment should be made in a time-bound framework and accountability should be fixed for any delay in way to extract maximum speed money from the beneficiaries.
2. Amount should be deposited in a fixed account for not less than a year. (Table 5B.5)

(d) Calculation of Poverty Indices :

Head-Count ratio :

$$H = \frac{q}{n} = \frac{31}{32} = 0.96875$$

Table 5B.5

Utilisation of Amount and General Observations

Zone	*Utilisation of the Amount*				*Beneficiary's Observation*	*Investigator's Observation*
	On consumption expenditure	*Undertaken a productive activity*	*Repayment of loan*	*Any other*		
North Bihar	03	02	04	00	1. Procedural delay should be avoided by simplification of the process.	1. Amount of speed money in the scheme is higher as the government pays Rs. 10000/ at a time.
Central Bihar	00	00	00	03	2. In case of death outside the local area, beneficiaries have to face a lot of problems in obtaining death	2. The authorities create a number of obstacles in case of no payment or less payment of speed money.
Jharkhand	07	06	07	00	certificate. This creates a lot of problems specifically in case of migrant labour	Suggestions : 1. The payment should be made in a time brand framework and accountability should be fixed for any delay
Total	10	08	11	03		in way to extract maximum speed money from the beneficiary. 2. Amount should be deposited in a fixed account for not less than a year.

FIG. 5B

Income Inequality for NFBS Beneficiaries

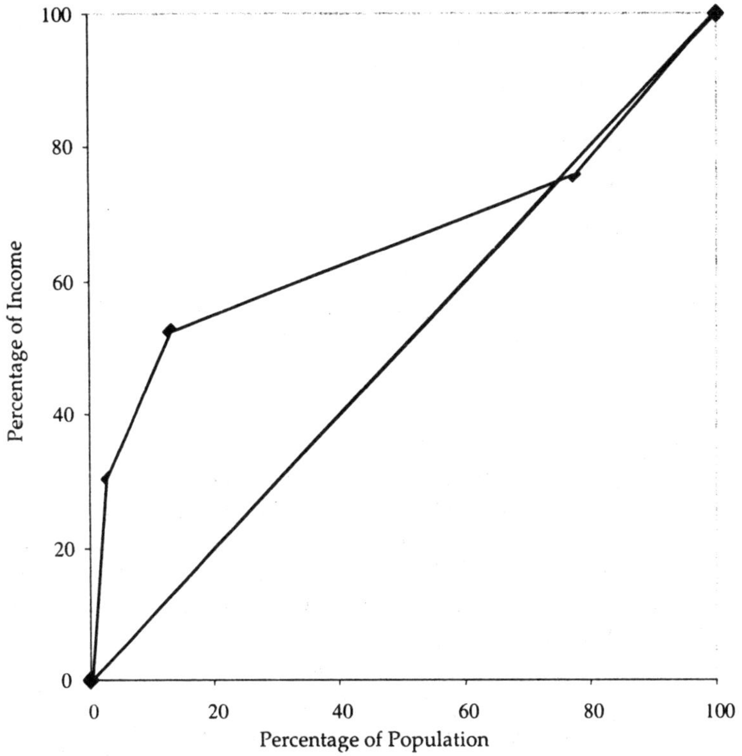

Percentage of Population	Percentage of Income
0	0
3.22	30.48
12.9	52.38
77.41	76.19
100	100

Income-Gap ratio :

$$I = \frac{g}{\pi . q} = \frac{216600}{21000x31} = 0.3327188$$

Ginni Co-efficient :

G = 0.16

Sen-Index (P)

P = H {I + (1-I) G}

= 0.97 [0.33 + (1-0.33) 0.16]

= 0.97 [0.33 + 0.67 x 0.16]

= 0.97 [0.33 + 0.11]

= 0.97 x 0.44

= 0.43

An Analysis of Poverty Index for the Scheme

The value of Head-Count Ratio (H) for the scheme reveals that 97% of the beneficiaries were below poverty line. The computed value of Income-gap ratio (I) viz. 0.33, shows that a considerable number of beneficiaries were in the upper income-slab below poverty line.

The value of Ginni co-efficient (G) is 0.16. In the calculation of G, the figure for Lorenz Curve shows that the number of beneficiaries in the income group Rs. 11000-16000 is so large that it even crosses the line of equality. This fact reduces the value of G. A lower value of G shows a low degree of income disparity among the beneficiaries below poverty line.

The figure for Sen-Index 0.43 signifies that the number of beneficiaries in upper income-slab below poverty line were relatively larger in number.

C. NATIONAL MATERNITY BENEFIT SCHEME (NMBS)

Under NMBS there is a provision for the payment of Rs. 500 per pregnancy to women belonging to poor households for pre-natal and post-natal maternity care upto first two live births. The benefit is provided to eligible women of 19 years and above. The effectiveness of the scheme had been evaluated under the study.

(a) Socio-economic Condition of Beneficiaries

Out of 60 (100%) female beneficiaries, only 20 (33.33%) were literate and 40 (66.66%) were illiterate beneficiaries 17 (85.0%) had the qualification of primary and above level but below matriculation level and only 3 (25.0%) had the qualification of matriculation and above level but below graduation level. North Bihar was totally lacking this level of education. On the other hand not a single beneficiary could reach upto graduation level. Out of 60 beneficiaries, 5 (8.33%) were small farmers. There was no small farmer in North Bihar. Only 2 (3.33%) hailing from only Central Bihar were marginal farmers. 11 (18.33%) were agricultural labourers, 12 (20.0%) were non-agricultural casual labourers, 18 (30.0%) were non-agricultural self-employed labourers who had taken the maximum benefit from the scheme. Only 2 (3.33%) were artisans and 10 (16.66%) hailing from only North Bihar were housewives. (Table 5C.1)

Out of 60 beneficiaries, 29 (48.33%) had the family size of 1-5 members, 28 (46.66%) had the family size of 6-11 members and only 3 (5.0%) had the size above 12 or more, but there was no family size of the same in Jharkhand. 27 (45.0%) beneficiaries belonged to scheduled castes, only 1 (1.66%) hailed from Jharkhand region belonged to scheduled tribes, 25 (41.66%) belonged to OBCs (North Bihar was lacking) and only 7 (11.66%) hailed from North Bihar belonged to others category. 3 (5.0%) beneficiaries only from Central Bihar were freed bonded labourers but there was no assignee of surplus land. Remaining 57 (95.0%) were others. (Table 5C.2)

Out of 60 beneficiaries only a single beneficiary from Jharkhand (1.66%) had income below Rs. 6401, 08 (13.33%) had income in between Rs. 6401-11000, 26 (43.33%) in between Rs. 11001-16000, 13 (21.66%) in between Rs. 16001-21000, 12 (20.0%) beneficiaries had income in between Rs. 21001-32000 and above. They were living above the poverty line. They had been able to manage to get the benefit from the scheme through manipulating skill. (Table - 5C.3)

TABLE 5C.1

Categorisation of Beneficiaries

Zone	*Sex*		*Literacy*		*Literacy Level*			*Beneficiary's Occupation at the Time of Selection*						
	Male	*Female*	*Literate*	*Illiterate*	*Primary & above*	*Matric & above*	*Graduation & above*	*SF*	*MF*	*Agri-Labour*	*Non-agri. Casual Labour*	*Non-agri. Self employed*	*Artisan*	*Others*
North Bihar	00	20	04	16	04	00	00	00	00	04	00	06	00	10
Central Bihar	00	20	05	15	04	01	00	04	02	05	01	07	01	00
Jharkhand	00	20	11	09	09	02	00	01	00	02	11	05	01	00
Total	00	60	20	40	17	03	00	05	02	11	12	18	02	10

TABLE 5C.2

Size of the Family and Social Classification

Zone	Size of the Family			Social Classification						
				Category I				Category II		
	1-5	6-11	12+	SC	ST	OBCs	Others	Ex/freed bonded labour	Assignies of surplus land	Others
North Bihar	11	7	02	13	00	00	07	00	00	20
Central Bihar	10	9	01	11	00	09	00	03	00	17
Jharkhand	08	12	00	03	01	16	00	00	00	20
Total	29	28	03	27	01	25	07	03	00	57

TABLE 5C.3

Family Income

Zone	*Below Poverty Line*			*Above Poverty Line*		
	Upto 6400	*6401-11000*	*11001-16000*	*16001-21000*	*21001-32000*	*32001+*
North Bihar	00	00	09	03	06	02
Central Bihar	00	04	06	06	01	03
Jharkhand	01	04	11	04	00	00
Total	01	08	26	13	07	05

(b) Economic Structure and Viability of the Scheme

The amount received by the female beneficiaries in all the zones was Rs. 500 per head. Out of 60 beneficiaries 51 (85.0%) reported that they had received the amount from the concerned block office, 1 (1.66%) from health Centre and 08 (13.33%) from any other sources whereas no one had reported to receive it from Panchayat office. Minimum 3.6 month had been taken in receiving the payment under the scheme after falling the application but the beneficiaries received the payment within 12.3 months after filing the application. The average gap between filing the application and receiving the payment was 7.8 months.

13 (21.66%) beneficiaries but not from Jharkhand reported that they had received the amount in the pre-natal maternity period and remaining 47 (78.33%) received the amount in the post-natal maternity period. (Table - 5C.4)

Out of 60 beneficiaries, 43 (71.66%) reported that they had paid the speed money whereas 17 (28.33%) had not paid any speed money 10 (23.25%) reported that they had paid below Rs. 51, 13 (30.23%) paid in between Rs. 51-100, 08 (18.60%) in between Rs. 101-150, other 08 (18.60%) in between Rs. 151-200 and only 4 (9.30%) paid above Rs. 201. It had been clear that the concerned Panchayat authority had taken no speed money, only 2 (4.76%) hailed only from Central Bihar had reported that the speed money had been appropriated by the concerned block authority, 9 (21.42%) reported that it had been appropriated by the middlemen, and 31 (73.80%) reported that it had been

TABLE 5C.4

Process of Assistance

Zone	*Amount Received*	*Source of Payment*				*Time taken in Payment after Filing Application (Months)*			*Amount Received for*	
		Block office	*Panchayat office*	*Health centre*	*Any other*	*Ave.*	*Min.*	*Max.*	*Pre natal maternity period*	*Post natal maternity period*
North Bihar	500	19	00	01	00	3.5	02	06	07	13
Central Bihar	500	20	00	00	00	5.4	03	07	06	14
Jharkhand	500	12	00	00	08	14.4	06	24	00	20
Total	1500	51	00	01	08	23.3	11	37	13	47

appropriated by others. (Table 5C.5)

39 (65.0%) beneficiaries reported that they had used the money for required purpose whereas 21 (35.0%) reported it negative. Out of this 21 beneficiaries, 18 (85.71%) reported that they had used the amount to face the challenges of poverty i.e., consumption requirements. 2 (9.52%) for loan repayment and only 1 (4.76%) for other purpose. Only a single beneficiary reported that the amount was adequate while the remaining 59 (98.33%) beneficiaries were of adverse views. The suggested minimum amount by the beneficiaries Rs. 2700 maximum amount was Rs. 9200 and average amount was Rs. 4500 in case of all the three zones. (Table 5C.6)

Out of 60 beneficiaries only 5 (8.33%) beneficiaries had only 1 male child, 5 (8.33%) beneficiaries had 2 male children, and 1 (1.66%) had only 3 male children. 11 (18.33%)beneficiaries had only 1 female child, 6 (10.0%) beneficiaries had only 2 female children and 3 (5.0%) beneficiaries had 3 female children. 13 (21.66%) beneficiaries had male and 1 female child and 15 (25.0%) beneficiaries had 3 male and female children. In case of 1 (1.66%) beneficiary the child did not remain alive. Out of 20 beneficiaries who had only female children, 14 (70.0%) had clearly shows a preference for male child but 6 (30.0%) had no opinion. Only 16 (26.66%) beneficiaries had received the assistance under he scheme earlier but 44 (73.33%) had taken the benefit of the scheme only once. Out of 16 beneficiaries who had received the assistance earlier also, 15 (93.75%) had received only once excluding the last assistance but 1 (6.25%) beneficiary had taken the benefit of the scheme twice excluding the last assistance.

(c) General Observations and Recommendations

Beneficiaries had observed that the amount was not adequate for them.

Investigators Observation/Suggestion about the Scheme

On the basis of cross-survey the Investigators had confirmed that

1. Assistance should be given in two parts, 50% in pre-natal period and 50% in post-natal period.

TABLE 5C.5

Speed Money

Zone	*Paid Speed Money for Inclusion in Pensioners List*		*Amount of Speed Money*						*Speed Money taken by:*			
	Yes	*No*	*0*	*1-50*	*51-100*	*101-150*	*151-200*	*200+*	*Block authority*	*Panchayat authority*	*Middle-man*	*Others*
North Bihar	04	16	16	00	00	00	04	00	00	00	04	00
Central Bihar	18	02	01	01	07	04	03	04	00	02	02	16
Jharkhand	20	00	00	09	06	04	01	00	00	00	03	17
Total	42	18	17	10	13	08	08	04	00	02	09	33

TABLE 5C.6

Use of Adequacy of Amount

Zone	*Amount used for Required Purpose*		*Reason for the Use of the Amount for Other Purpose*			*Amount is Adequate*		*Suggested Adequate Amount*		
	Yes	*No*	*Poverty and consumption requirements*	*Loan Repayment*	*Any other*	*Yes*	*No*	*Min.*	*Max.*	*Ave.*
North Bihar	16	04	02	01	00	00	20	1000	2700	1500
Central Bihar	14	06	04	01	01	01	19	700	2000	1250
Jharkhand	09	11	11	00	00	00	20	1000	4500	1750
Total	39	21	17	02	01	01	59	2700	9200	4500

TABLE 5C.7

Preference for Male Child

Zone	No. Children									In Case of only Female Child/Children has the Beneficiary a Perference for			Has Beneficiary Received Assistance under the Scheme Period to this		How many Times the Beneficiary Received Assistance and the Programme, Piror to this			
	Only male			Only female			Both		No child (not alive/ unborn)	Yes	No	No opinion	Yes	No	0	1	2	3+
	1	2	3+	1	2	3+	2	3+										
North Bihar	01	02	01	05	02	00	06	03	00	02	00	05	08	12	00	08	00	00
Central Bihar	03	02	00	06	02	02	01	03	01	10	00	00	04	16	00	03	01	00
Jharkhand	01	01	00	00	02	01	06	09	00	02	00	01	04	16	00	04	00	00
Total	05	05	01	11	06	03	13	15	01	14	00	06	16	44	00	15	01	00

TABLE 5C.8

General Observations

Zone	*Beneficiary's Observation about the Scheme*	*Investigator's Observatins/ Suggestions about the Scheme*
North Bihar	1. Amount not adequate	1. Assistance should be given in two parts. 50% in pre natal period and 50% in post natal period. 2. Higher post natal assistance should be given in case of female child. 3. Amount should be given through cheque, not in case to avoid corruption. 4. The cheque must be account payee in a bank or post office for proper utilisaiton of the amount. 5. Strict action should be taken in case of any complain. 6. Strict action should be taken in case of payment to the persons of affluent section.

2. Higher post-natal assistance should be given in case of female child.
3. Amount should be given through cheque to avoid corruption.
4. The cheque must be account payee in a Bank or Post office for proper utilisation of the amount.
5. Strict action should be taken in case of any complaint.
6. Strict action should be taken in case of payment to the persons of the affluent sections of society.

(d) Calculation of Poverty Indices

Head-Count ratio :

$$H = \frac{q}{n} = \frac{48}{60} = 0.80$$

FIG. 5C

Income Inequality for NMBS Beneficiaries

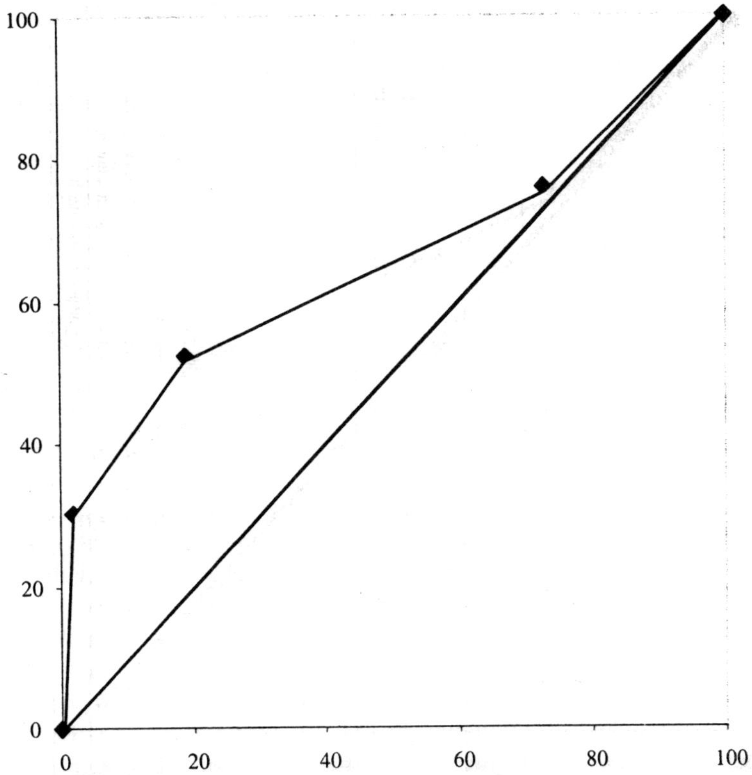

Percentage of Population	Percentage of Income
0	0
2.08	30.48
18.74	52.38
72.8	76.19
100	100

Income-Gap ratio :

$$I = \frac{g}{\pi.q} = \frac{351000}{21000x48} = 0.3482142$$

Ginni Co-efficient :

$G = 0.16$

Sen-Index :

$P = H \{I + (1-I) G\}$

$= 0.80 [0.35 + (1-0.35) 0.16]$

$= 0.80 [0.35 + 0.65 \times 0.16]$

$= 0.80 [0.35 + 0.10]$

$= 0.80 \times 0.45$

$= 0.36$

An Analysis of Poverty Index for the Scheme

The Head-Count Ratio (H) for the scheme NMBS shows that 80% of the beneficiaries were below poverty line. The value of Income gap ratio viz. 0.35 implies that most of the beneficiaries were in the upper income-slab below poverty line.

In the calculation of Sen-index the value of Ginni co-efficient (G) is 0.16. which signifies a very low degree of income disparity among the beneficiaries below poverty line. The Sen-index value, viz. 0.36 indicates that more beneficiaries were in the upper income-slab below poverty line.

CHAPTER

6

AN EPILOGUE

The study has confirmed that the poverty alleviation programmes have not made any significant dent on the problem of poverty. Poverty of poverty alleviation programmes jointly with anti development institutional frame work have successfully kept the poverty intact. The abject poverty is prevalent over the system in tune with the global counterparts with the following characteristics :

1. Lack of income and assets to attain basic necessities—food, shelter, clothing and acceptable level of health and education.
2. Sense of voicelessness and powerlessness in the institutions of state and society.
3. Vulnerability to adverse shocks, linked to an inability to cope with them (World Bank 2000/2001).

The study has revealed the following :

(i) 24.0% beneficiaries of poverty alleviation programmes have income above poverty line, despite that they have taken the benefit of the schemes through their manipulating skills.
(ii) A large proportion of beneficiaries are in the upper income-slab below poverty line in all the survey

zones and schemes. Sen-Index has confirmed it in case of the zones and the schemes earlier.

(iii) Poverty alleviation schemes have been implemented only on paper to misutilise the resources in significant proportion.

(iv) All the poverty alleviation schemes in all the zones have been deeply influenced by payment of speed money. In other words, the payment of speed money has been an essential condition for getting the benefit of anti-poverty schemes with few exceptions.

(v) Neither the authorities nor the beneficiaries have taken the schemes in their true spirit. The authorities have taken it as a source of additional resource mobilisation for their own and subject to complete mere formalities. The beneficiaries have taken the assistance as a subsidy without any serious thought on the purpose of the assistance and the possibilities.

(vi) No system could be evolved for mass awareness about the poverty alleviation schemes. The amount received under the scheme have been siphoned off in collaboration with the concerned authorities and the local power brokers/middlemen due to unawareness of the common masses.

Poverty alleviation schemes have been implemented in the form of distribution of alms without any serious consideration to generate viable income or service.

(vii) Procedural delay/bureaucratic red-tapism has been a common feature in execution of poverty alleviation programmes.

(viii) NGOs and PRIs have played no role in the implementation of poverty alleviation schemes. PRIs have been completely defunct in the state as no election was held in between 1978 and 2000.

Schemes for direct attack on poverty were introduced to supplement/complement the mainstream of development effort under the *trickle-down hypothesis*. Slow rate of growth of the economy alongwith maintained population growth rate had necessitated to go for direct attack on poverty. But the empirical evaluation of the poverty alleviation programmes, i.e., direct attack on poverty reveals that the significant proportion of the schemes had been misutilised in the name of poverty alleviation. Abject poverty has been considered as a good politics and scarce resources were wasted mercilessly without reaching the poor.

Poverty cannot be alleviated in a fragmented cartesian manner. A holistic approach is required to break the Neo vicious circle of poverty. Half-hearted, faltering and piece-meal efforts may be a good politics but a bad economics. In this background the following recommendations are propounded for a structural transformation of the system :

(i) Schemes must have viable income generating potentials. Without consideration of viable income, no scheme should be undertaken to misuse the scarce resources.

(ii) Transparent and time-bound implementation procedure should be evolved and tendency of concerned authorities and power brokers to siphon off the funds of the schemes should be effectively curbed.

(iii) Without raising the honest and efficient administrative level no qualitative break would be possible in the system. A viable policy for the metamorphosis of the economic administration should be evolved.

(iv) Resources should be allocated for primary education specially for job-oriented education which would generate maximum total linkage effect in the system.

(v) Health facilities should be improved and special attention should be given on family based welfare measure to reduce the population pressure.

(vi) NGOs should be assigned dynamic role in the process of poverty alleviation specially in the field of mass education and mass awareness.

(vii) Effective decentralized system should be strengthened by making the Panchayati Raj

Institutions (PRIs) functional.

(viii) Pragmatic decision should be taken to salvage the system from the traps of Crime-Syndicates functioning in perfect nexus with bureaucracy, policy, politicians and mafias to siphon off any type of resources with chickenery methods.

Participatory Monitoring of the Process of Social Mobilisation for Poverty Alleviation

SOCIOGRAM

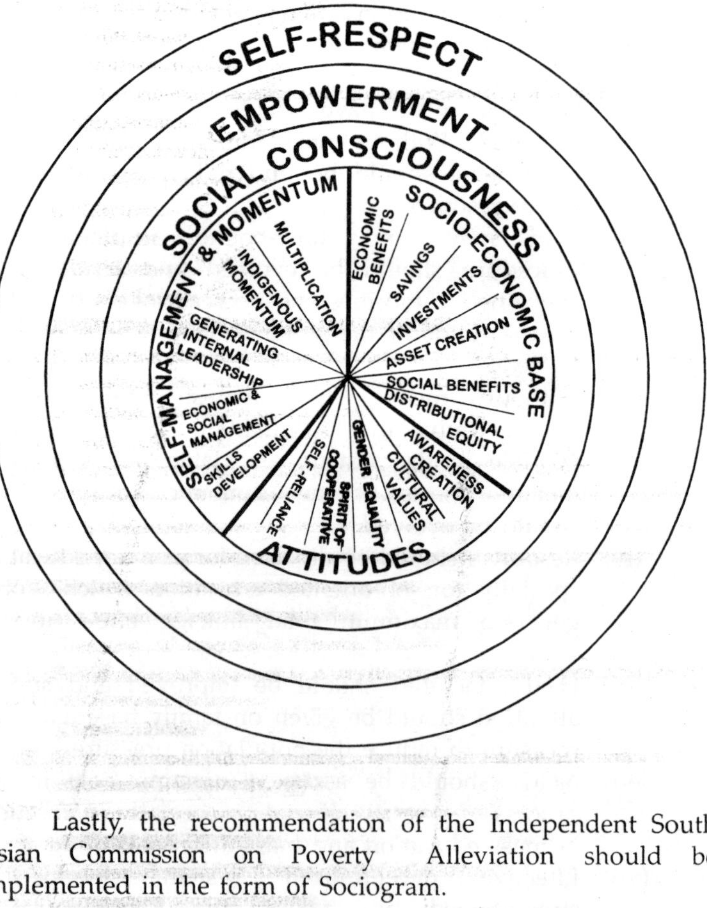

Lastly, the recommendation of the Independent South Asian Commission on Poverty Alleviation should be implemented in the form of Sociogram.

The criteria in the Sociogram are all interrelated and mutually reinforcing. However, they deserve to be presented separately not only for their own sake but more importantly, because they contribute to each other's growth and thereby to the total process. If one element in the process is not moving forward it can easily be identified and strengthened. The three major planks that deepen social consciousness and lead to the empowerment of the poor are attitudinal change, the capacity for self-management and the economic and social base of the poor. It is axiomatic that the economic base of the poor has to be improved over a period of time through a dual process of savings investment and asset creation and the emancipation of the poor from economic and social bondage, to enable them not only to be more productive and keep the surplus in their own hands. The establishment of a self-reliant activity base will mutually reinforce the process of promoting positive attitudinal values. Conscious attempts to diagnose, assess and mutually stimulate such values will bring them to the fore and will contribute to turning them into a driving force for further action, contributing to a deepening expansion of the process itself. Ultimately the process as a whole, which starts with the release of the creativity of the poor, has to be judged by the increase in their social consciousness, empowerment and self-respect. It would have the way to break the Neo-Vicious Circle of Poverty (Vicious Circle of Poverty under institutional framework) and initiate the virtuous circle of development.

TECHNICAL NOTE

The commonest measure of over-all poverty is the head-count measure H, given by the proportion of the total population that happens to be identified as poor, e.g. as falling below the specified poverty line income. If q be the number of people who are identified as being poor and n the total number of people in the community, then the head- count measure H is simply q/n.

Another measure that has had a fair amount of currency is the so-called 'poverty-gap', which is the aggregate shortfall of income of all the poor from the specified poverty line. The index can be normalized by being expressed as the percentage short fall of the average income of the poor from the poverty line.

This measure denoted by—I will be called the 'Income gap ratio'.

The income gap ratio—I is completely insensitive to transfers of income among the poor so long as nobody crosses the poverty line by such transfers. It also pays no attention whatever be the number or proportion of poor people below the poverty line, concentrating only on the aggregate short fall, no matter how it is distributed and among how many. These are damaging limitations.

The head-count measure H is, of course, not insensitive to the number below the poverty line; indeed, for a given society it is the only thing to which H is sensitive. But H pays no attention whatever to the extent of income short fall of those who lie below the poverty line. It matters not to all whether someone is just below the line or very far from it in acute misery and hunger.

Furthermore, a transfer of income from a poor person to one who is richer can never increase the poverty measure H surely is perverse feature. The poor person from whom the transfer takes place is, in any case, counted in the value of H, and no reduction of his income will make him count any more than he does already. On the other hand, the person who receives the income transfer cannot, of course, move below the poverty line as a consequence of this. Either he was rich and stays so or was poor and stays so, in both of which cases the measure H remains unaffected; or he was below the line but is pulled above it by the transfer, and this makes the measure H fall rather than rise. So a transfer from a poor person to one who is richer can never increase poverty as represented by H.

The head-count measure H ignores the extent of income short falls, while the income gap ratio I ignores the numbers involved : why not a combination of the two ? This is, alas, still inadequate, If a unit of income is transferred from a person below the poverty line to some one who is richer but who still is (and remains) below the poverty line, then both the measures H and I will remain completely unaffected. Hence any 'combined' measure based only on these two must also show no response whatsoever to such a change, despite the obvious increase in aggregate poverty as a consequence of this transfer in terms of relative deprivation.

There is, however, a special case in which a combination of H and I might just about be adequate. If we were, to confine ourselves to cases in which all the poor have precisely the same income, it may be reasonable to expect that H and I together may do the job. Transfers of the kind that have been considered above to show the insensitivity of the combination of H and I will not then be in the domain of our discourse.

Amartya Sen gave an alternative poverty index to overcome the limitations of H & I. He took the poverty measure being a weighted sum of income gaps. When G is the Ginni coefficient of the distribution of income among the poor, this measure is given by $P = H \{I + (1-I)G\}$. When all the poor have the same income, then the Ginni coefficient G of income distribution among the poor equals zero, and P equals HI. Given the same average poverty gap and the same proportion of poor population in total population, the poverty measure P increases with greater inequity of income below the poverty line, as measured by the Ginni co-efficient. Thus, the measure

P is a function of H (reflecting the number of poor), I (reflecting the aggregate poverty gap), and G (reflecting the inequality of income distribution below the poverty line). The last captures the aspect of 'relative deprivation', and its inclusion is indeed a direct consequence of the axiom of Ranked Relative Deprivation which focuses on the distribution of income among the poor.

(d) Calculation of Poverty Indices

Head-count ratio (H)

$$H = \frac{q}{n},$$

where q = No. of beneficiaries below poverty line
n = Total number of beneficiaries.

Income-gap ratio (I)

$$I = \frac{g}{\pi . q},$$

where $g = \sum_{i=1}^{n} g_i$ (the aggregate poverty gap)

where $g_i = p - y_i$
p = Poverty line income (Rs. 21,000 at current prices)
Y_i = Income of the ith beneficiary.

Ginni Co-efficient (G)

$$G = \frac{\text{Area of the shaded region (see graph)}}{\text{Area of the triangle above poverty line}}$$

Area of the shaded region is calculated by using the formula for the calculation of area of a polygon

Area of a polygon whose vertices taken in order are (x_1, y_1), (x_2, y_2), (x_3, y_3) ... (x_n, y_n) is given by -

$$\Rightarrow = \frac{1}{2}\left[\begin{vmatrix} x_1 & y_1 \\ x_2 & y_2 \end{vmatrix} + \begin{vmatrix} x_2 & y_2 \\ x_3 & y_3 \end{vmatrix} + \ldots\ldots + \begin{vmatrix} x_n & y_n \\ x_1 & y_1 \end{vmatrix}\right]$$

After calculation of area the modulus values are taken.

The calculation of Ginni co-efficient has been made by drawing the Lorenz Curve showing income inequality between the cumulative percentage of beneficiaries on the horizontal axis and the cumulative percentage of income at/below poverty line on the vertical axis.

The percentage figure for income has been calculated by assuming poverty line income, at Rs. 21000 at current prices, as 100. The different percentage figures were calculated by taking the upper limits of the different income slabs under which the beneficiaries are identified and then the percentage data are cumulated. Similarly, the number of beneficiaries under different income slabs were put into percentage figure by taking the total number of beneficiaries as 100 and then the data are cumulated.

Sen-Index (P)

$$P = H \{ I + (1 - I) G \}$$

ANNEXURE TABLE 1

Poverty—The Global Scenario

Economy	*Population Millions 1999*	*Surface area Thousands of sq. km 1999*	*Survey year*	*National poverty lines: Population below the poverty line (%) Rural*	*Urban*	*National*	*Survey year*	*Population below the Rural*	*Urban*	*National*	*Survey*	*International poverty line: Population below $1 a day %*	*Population gap $1 a day %*	*Population gap $2 a day %*	*Population gap $1 a day %*
1	2	3	4	5	6	7	8	9	10	11	12	13	44	15	16
Albania	3	29	—	..	..	..		..	..	..		..	..	..	..
Algeria	30	2,382	1988	16.6	7.3	12.2	1995	30.3	14.7	22.6	1995	<2	<0.5	15.1	3.6
Angola	12	1,247	—	..	..	..		..	..	..		..	..	..	..
Argentina	37	2,780	1991	..	..	25.5	1993	..	..	17.6		..	..	..	..
Armenia	4	30	—	..	..	..		..	..	..		..	..	..	..
Australia	19	7,741	—	..	..	..		..	..	..		..	..	..	..
Austria	8	84	—	..	..	..		..	..	..		..	..	..	..
Azerbaijan	8	87	1995	..	..	68.1		..	..	..		..	..	..	..
Bangladesh	128	144	1991-92	46.0	23.3	42.7	1995-96	39.8	14.3	35.6	1996	29.1	5.9	77.8	31.8
Belarus	10	208	1995	..	..	22.5		..	..	..	1998	<2	<0.5	<2	0.1
Belgium	10	33	—	..	..	..		..	..	..		..	..	..	..
Benin	6	113	1995	..	..	33.0		..	..	..		..	..	..	..
Bolivia	8	1,099	1993	..	29.3	..	1995	79.1	..	..	1990	11.3	2.2	38.6	13.5
Botswana	2	582	—	..	..	..		..	..	..	1985-86	33.3	12.5	61.4	30.7
Brazil	168	8,547	1990	32.6	13.1	17.4		..	..	..	1997	5.1	1.3	17.4	6.3

Bulgaria	8	111	—	..	..	..		..	..	..	1995	<2	<0.5	7.8	1.6
Burkina Faso	11	274	—	..	..	..		..	..	..	1994	61.2	25.5	85.8	50.9
Burundi	7	28	1990	..	..	36.2		..	..	..		..	..	..	..
Cambodia	12	181	1993-94	43.1	24.8	39.0	1997	40.1	21.1	36.1		..	..	..	..
Cameroon	15	475	1984	32.4	44.4	40.0		..	..	..		..	..	..	..
Canada	31	9,971	—	..	..	..		..	..	..		..	..	..	..
Central African Republic	4	623	—	..	..	..		..	..	..	1993	66.6	38.1	84.0	58.4
Chad	7	1,284	1995-96	67	63	64.0		..	..	..		..	..	..	..
Chile	15	757	1992	..		21.6	1994	..	..	20.5	1994	4.2	0.7	20.3	5.9
China	1,250	9,597	1996	7.9	2	6.0	1998	4.6	<2	4.6	1998	18.5	4.2	53.7	21.0
Hong Kong, China	7	1	—	..	..	..		..	..	..		..	..	..	..
Colombia	42	1,139	1991	29.0	7.8	16.9	1992	31.2	8.0	17.7	1996	11.0	3.2	28.7	11.6
Congo, Dem. Rep.	50	2,345	—	..	..	..		..	..	..		..	..	..	..
Congo, Rep.	3	342	—	..	..	..		..	..	..		..	..	..	..
Costa Rica	4	51	—	..	..	..		..	..	..	1996	9.6	3.2	26.3	10.1
Cote d'Ivoire	15	322	—	..	..	..		..	..	..	1995	12.3	2.4	49.4	16.8
Croatia	4	57	—	..	..	..		..	..	..		..	..	..	..
Czech Republic	10	79	—	..	..	..		..	..	..	1993	<2	<0.5	<2	<0.5
Denmark	5	43	—	..	..	..		..	..	..		..	..	..	..
Dominican Republic	8	49	1989	27.4	23.3	24.5	1992	29.8	10.9	20.6	1996	3.2	0.7	16.0	5.0
Ecuador	12	284	1994	47	25	35		..	..	..	1995	20.2	5.8	52.3	21.2
Egypt, Arab Rep.	62	1,001	1995-96	23.3	22.5	22.9		..	..	..	1995	3.1	0.3	52.7	11.4
El Salvador	6	21	1992	55.7	43.1	48.3		..	..	..	1996	25.3	10.4	51.9	24.7
Eritrea	4	118	—	..		..		..	..	..		..	..	..	..
Estonia	1	45	1995	14.7	6.8	8.9		..	..	..	1995	4.9	1.2	17.7	6.0

(Contd.)

ANNEXURE TABLE 1 *(Contd.)*

1	2	3	4	5	6	7	8	9	10	11	12	13	44	15	16
Ethiopia	63	1,104	—	..	..	..		..	..	..	1995	31.3	8.0	76.4	32.9
Finland	5	338	—	..	..	..		..	..	..		..	..	..	..
France	59	552	—	..	..	..		..	..	..		..	..	..	..
Georgia	5	70	1997	9.9	12.1	11.1		..	..	..		..	..	..	..
Germany	82	357	—		..	..		..	..	..		..	..	..	..
Ghana	19	239	1992	34.3	26.7	31.4		..	..	..		..	..	..	..
Greece	11	132	—		..	..		..	..	..		..	..	..	..
Guatemala	11	109	1989	71.9	33.7	57.9		..	..	..	1989	39.8	19.8	64.3	36.6
Guinea	7	246	1994	..	..	40.0		..	..	..		..	..	..	..
Haiti	8	28	1987	..	..	65.0	1995	66.0	..	..		..	..	..	..
Honduras	6	112	1992	46.0	56.0	50.0	1993	51.0	57.0	53.0	1996	40.5	17.5	68.8	36.9
Hungary	10	93	1989	..	..	1.6	1993	..	..	8.6	1993	<2	<0.5	4.0	0.9
India	998	3,288	1992	43.5	33.7	40.9	1994	36.7	30.5	35.0	1997	44.2	12.0	86.2	41.4
Indonesia	207	1,905	1996	12.3	9.7	11.3	1998	22.0	17.8	20.3	1999	15.2	2.5	66.1	22.6
Iran, Islamic Rep.	63	1,633	—	..	..	..		..	..	..		..	..	..	..
Ireland	4	70	—	..	..	..		..	..	..		..	..	..	..
Israel	6	21	—	..	..	..		..	..	..		..	..	..	..
Italy	58	301	—	..	..	..		..	..	..		..	..	..	..
Jamaica	3	11	1992	..	..	34.2		..	..	..	1996	3.2	0.7	25.2	6.9
Japan	127	378	—	..	..	..		..	..	..		..	..	..	..
Jordan	5	89	1991	..	..	15.00	1997	..	..	11.7	1997	<2	<0.5	7.40	1.40
Kazakhstan	15	2717	1996	39.0	30.0	34.6		..	..	..	1996	1.50	0.30	15.30	3.90
Kenya	29	586	1992	46.4	29.3	42.0		..	..	..	1994	26.50	9.00	62.30	27.50

Korea, Rep.	47	99		..	..	..		..	..	..	1993	<2	<0.5	<2	<0.5
Kuwait	2	18		..	..	..		..	..	..		..	..	..	..
Kyrgyz Republic	5	199	1993	48.1	28.7	40.0	1997	64.5	28.5	51.0		..	..	..	..
Lao PDR	5	237	1993	53.0	24.0	46.1		..	..	..		..	..	..	..
Latvia	2	66		..	..	..		..	..	..	1998	<2	<0.5	8.30	2.00
Lebanon	4	10		..	..	..		..	..	..		..	..	..	..
Lesotho	2	30	1993	53.9	27.8	49.2		..	..	..	1993	43.10	20.30	65.70	38.10
Lithuania	4	65		..	..	..		..	..	..	1996	<2	<0.5	7.80	2.00
Macedonia, FYR	2	26		..	..	..		..	..	..		..	..	..	..
Madogascar	15	587	1993-94	77.0	47.0	70.0	1995	..	..	..	1993	60.20	24.50	88.80	51.30
Malawi	11	118	1990-91	..	..	54.0		..	..	..		..	..	..	..
Malaysia	23	330	1989	..	..	15.5		..	..	..		..	..	..	..
Mali	11	1240		..	..	..		..	..	..	1994	72.80	37.40	90.60	60.50
Mauritania	3	1026	1989-90	..	..	57.0		..	..	..	1995	3.80	1.00	22.10	6.60
Mexico	97	1958	1988	..	..	10.1		..	..	..	1995	17.90	6.10	42.50	18.10
Moldova	4	34	1997	26.7	..	23.3		..	..	..	1992	7.30	1.30	31.90	10.20
Mongolia	3	1567	1995	33.1	38.5	36.3		..	..	..	1995	13.90	3.10	50.00	17.50
Morocco	28	447	1990-91	18.0	7.6	13.1	1989-99	27.2	12.0	19.0	1990-91	<2	<0.5	7.50	1.30
Mozambigue	17	802		..	..	..		..	..	..	1996	37.90	12.00	78.40	36.80
Myanmar	45	677		..	..	..		..	..	..		..	..	..	..
Namibia	2	824		..	..	..		..	..	..	1993	34.90	14.00	55.80	30.40
Nepal	23	147	1995-96	44.0	23.0	42.0		..	..	..	1995	37.70	9.70	82.50	37.50
Netherlands	16	41		..	..	..		..	..	..		..	..	..	..
New Zealand	4	271		..	..	..		..	..	..		..	..	..	..
Nicaragua	5	130	1993	76.1	31.9	50.3		..	..	..		..	..	..	..
Niger	10	1267	1989-93	66.0	52.0	63.0		..	..	..	1995	61.40	33.90	85.30	54.80

(Contd.)

ANNEXURE TABLE 1 *(Contd.)*

1	2	3	4	5	6	7	8	9	10	11	12	13	44	15	16
Nigeria	124	924	1985	49.5	31.7	43.0	1992-93	36.4	30.4	34.1	1997	70.20	34.90	90.80	59.00
Norway	4	324		..	..	..		..	..	..		..	..	..	..
Pakistan	135	796	1991	36.9	28.0	34.0		..	..	..	1996	31.00	6.20	84.70	35.00
Panama	3	76	1997	64.9	15.3	37.3		..	..	..	1997	10.30	3.20	25.10	10.20
Papua, New Guinea	5	463		..	..	..		..	..	..		..	..	..	..
Paraguay	5	407	1991	28.5	19.7	21.8		..	..	..	1995	19.40	8.30	38.50	18.80
Peru	25	1285	1994	67.0	46.1	53.5	1997	64.7	40.4	49.0	1996	15.50	5.40	41.40	17.10
Philippines	77	300	1994	53.1	28.0	40.6	1997	51.2	22.5	40.6		..	..	..	..
Poland	39	323	1993	..	..	23.8		..	..	..	1993	5.40	4.30	10.50	6.00
Portugal	10	92		..	..	..		..	..	..	1994	<2	<0.5	<2	<0.5
Romania	22	238	1994	27.9	20.4	21.5		..	..	..	1994	2.80	0.80	27.50	6.90
Russain Federation	147	17075	1994	..	..	30.9		..	..	..	1998	7.10	1.40	25.10	8.70
Rwanda	8	26	1993	..	..	51.2		..	..	..	1983-85	35.70	7.70	84.60	36.70
Saudi Arabia	21	2150		..	..	..		..	..	..		..	..	..	..
Senegal	9	197		..	..	..		..	..	..	1995	26.30	7.00	67.80	28.20
Sierra Leone	5	72	1989	76.0	53.0	68.0		..	..	..	1989	57.00	39.50	74.50	51.80
Singapore	3	1		..	..	..		..	..	..		..	..	..	..
Slovak Republic	5	49		..	..	..		..	..	..	1992	<2	<0.5	<2	<0.5
Slovenia	2	20		..	..	..		..	..	..	1993	<2	<0.5	<2	<0.5
South Africa	42	1221		..	..	..		..	..	..	1993	11.50	1.80	35.80	13.40
Spain	39	506		..	..	..		..	..	..		..	..	..	..
Sri Lanka	19	66	1985-86	45.5	26.8	40.6	1990-91	38.1	28.4	35.3	1995	6.60	1.00	45.40	13.50
Sweden	9	450		..	..	..		..	..	..		..	..	..	..

Switzerland	7	41		..	..	..		..	..	..		..	..	..	..
Syram Arab Republic	16	185		..	..	..		..	..	..		..	..	..	..
Tajikistan	6	143		..	..	..		..	..	..		..	..	..	..
Tanzania	33	945	1991	..	..	51.1		..	..	..	1993	19.90	4.80	59.70	23.00
Thailand	62	513	1990	..	..	18.0	1992	15.5	10.2	13.1	1998	<2	<0.5	28.20	7.10
Togo	5	57	1987-89	..	..	32.3		..	..	..		..	..	..	..
Tunisia	9	164	1985	29.2	12.0	19.9	1990	21.6	8.9	14.1	1990	<2	<0.5	11.60	2.90
Turkey	64	775		..	..	..		..	..	..	1994	2.40	0.50	18.00	5.00
Turkmensistan	5	488		..	..			..	..	..	1993	20.90	5.70	59.00	23.30
Uganda	21	241	1993	..	..	55.0		..	..	..	1992	36.70	11.40	77.20	35.80
Ukraine	50	604	1995	..	..	31.7		..	..	..	1996	<2	<0.5	23.70	4.40
United Kingdom	59	245		..	..	..		..	..	..		..	..	..	..
United States	273	9364		..	..	..		..	..	..		..	..	..	..
Uniguay	3	177		..	..	..		..	..	..	1989	<2	<0.5	6.60	1.90
Uzbekistan	25	447		..	..	..		..	..	..	1993	3.30	0.50	26.50	7.30
Venezuela, RB	24	912	1989	..	..	31.3		..	..	..	1996	14.70	5.60	36.40	15.70
Vietnam	78	332	1993	57.2	25.9	50.9		..	..	..		..	..	..	..
Yemen, Rep.	17	528	1992	19.2	18.6	19.1		..	..	..	1998	5.10	0.90	35.50	10.10
Zambia	10	753	1991	88.0	46.0	68.0	1993	..	..	86.0	1996	72.60	37.70	91.70	61.20
Zimbabwe	12	391	1990-91	31.0	10.0	25.5		..	..	..	1990-91	36.00	9.60	64.20	29.40

Annexure Table 2

Classification of Economics by Income and Region, 2000

Income group	*Sub-group*	*Sub-Saharan Africa*		*Asia*		*Europe and Central Asia*		*Middle East and North Africa*		
		East and Southern Africa	*West Africa*	*East Asia and Pacific*	*South Asia*	*Eastern Europe and Central Asia*	*Rest of Europe*	*Middle East*	*North Africa*	*Americas*
1	2	3	4	5	6	7	8	9	10	11
Low income		Angola Burundi Comoros Congo, Dem, Rep. Eritrea Ethiopia Kenya Lesotho Madagascar Malawi Mazambique Rwamda Somalia Sudan Tanznia Ugande Zambia Zimbabwe	Benin Burkina Faso Cameroon Central African Republic Chad Congo, Rep. Cote d'Ivoire Gambia, The Ghana Guinea Guinea-Bissau Liberia Mali Mauritania Niger Nigeria Sao Tome and Principe	Cambodia Indonesia Korea, Dem. Rep. Lao PDR Mongolia Myanmar Solomon Islands Vietnam	Afghanistan Bangladesh Bhutan India Nepal Pakistan	Armenia Azerbaijan Georgia Kyrgyz Republic Moldova Tajikistan Turkmenistan Ukraine Uzbekistan		Yemen, Rep.		Haiti Nicaragua

			Senegal Sierra Leone Togo							
Middle Income	Lower	Namibia Swaziland	Cape Verde Equatorial Guinea	China Fiji Kiribati Marshall Islands Micronesia Fed. Sts. Papua New Guinea Philippines Samoa Thailand Tonga Vanuatu	Maldives Sri Lanka	Albania Belarus Bosnia and Herzegovina Bulgaria Kazakhstan Latvia Lithuania Macedonia, FYR Romania Russian Federation Yugoslavia Fed. Rep.	Turkey	Iran, Islamic Rep. Iraq Jordan Syrian Arab Republic West Bank and Gaza	Algeria Djibouti Eqypt, Arab Rep. Morocco Tonisia	Belize Bolivia Colombia Costa Rica Cuba Dominican Republic Ecuador El Salvador Guatemale Guyana Honduras Jamaica Paraguay Peru St. Vincent and The Grenadines Suriname
	Upper	Bitswaba Mauritius Mayotte Seychelles South Africa	Gabon	American Samoa Korea, Rep. Malaysia Palau		Croatia Crech Republic Estonia Hungary Poland	Isle of Man	Bahrain Lebanon Oman Saudi Arabia	Libya Malta	Antigua and Barbuda Argentina Barbados Brazil Chile

(Contd.)

ANNEXURE TABLE 2 (*Contd.*)

1	2	3	4	5	6	7	8	9	10	11
						Slovak Republic				Dominica Grenada Mexico Panama Puerto Rico St. Kitts and Novis St. Lucia Trinidad and Tobago Uruguay, Venezuela, RB
	OECD			Australia Japan New Zealand			Austria Belgium Denmark Finland France Germany Greece Iceland Ireland Italy Luxembourg Netherlands Norway Portugal			Canada United States

							Spain Sweden Switzerland United Kingdom			
High Income	Non-OECD			Brunei French Polynesia Guam Hong Kong China Macao China New Caledonia N. Mariana Islands Singapore Taiwan China		Slovenia	Andorra Chennei Islands Cyprus Faeroe Islands Greenland Liechtenstein Monaco	Israel Kuwait Qatar United Arab Emirates		Aruba Bahamas, The Bermuda Cayman Islands Netherlands Antilles Virgin Islands (U.S.)
Total	157	25	23	23	8	25	2	10	7	33

Source: World Development Report 2000-2001.

ANNEXURE TABLE 3

Human Poverty in Developing Countries

HDI rank	Human poverty index (HPI-1) 1998		People not expected to survive to age 40† (%) a 1998	Adult illiteracy rate† (%age 15 and above) 1998	Population without access			Under weight children under age five† (%) 1990-1998b	Share of income or consumption			Population below income poverty line (%)	
	Rank	Value (%)			To safe water† (%) 1990-1998b	To health services† (%) 1981-1998b	To sanitation (%) 1990-1998b		Poorest 20% (%) 1987-1998b	Richest 20% (%) 1987-1998b	Richest 20% to poorest 1987-1998b	$1 a day (1993 PPP US $) 1989-1998b	National poverty line 1987-1997b
1	2	3	4	5	6	7	8	9	10	11	12	13	14
High human development													
22 Cyprus	..	..	3.2	3.4	0	0	..	..	..	..	..	..	..
24 Singapore	..	..	2.2	8.2	0 c	0	..	..	..	..	..	..	..
26 Hong Kong, China (SAR)	..	..	2.2	7.1	..	..	..	..	..	..	..	..	..
30 Barbados	..	..	3.1	..	0	0	0	5 c	..	..	..	..	..
31 Korea, Rep. of	..	..	4.6	2.5	7	0	0	..	7.5	39.3	5.2	..	..
32 Brunei Darussalam	..	..	3.1	9.3	..	4	..	..	..	..	..	..	..
33 Bahamas	..	..	5.7	4.5	6	0	18	..	..	..	..	..	..
35 Argentina	..	..	5.5	3.3	29	..	32	..	..	..	..	..	25.5

36 Kuwait	..	..	2.8	19.1	..	0	..	6 c	..	..	..	..	..
37 Antigua and Barbuda	..	..	..	..	..	0	4	10 c	..	..	..	..	..
38 Chile	4	4.7	4.4	4.6	9	5	..	1	3.5	61.0	17.4	4.2	20.5
39 Uruguay	1	3.9	5	2.4	5 c, d	0 c	..	5	5.4	48.3	8.9	6.6 e	..
41 Bahrain	9	9.6	4.6	13.5	6	0	3	9	..	..	..	..	..
42 Qatar	17	13.7	4.8	19.6	0 f	0	3	6	..	..	..	..	..
45 United Arab-Emirates	28	17.9	3	25.4	3	10	8	14	..	..	..	..	..
Medium human development													
47 Saint Kitts and Nevis	..	..	..	..	0	0	0	..	..	..	..	..	..
48 Costa Rica	2	4	3.9	4.7	4	3	16	2	4.0	51.8	13.0	9.6	..
50 Trinidad and Tobago	5	5.1	4	6.6	3	1	..	7 c	5.5	45.9	8.3	12.4	21.0
51 Dominica	..	..	..	..	4	0	20	5 c	..	..	..	..	..
53 Seychelles	..	..	..	..	..	1	..	6 c	..	..	..	..	..
54 Grenada	..	..	..	..	..	..	..	..	..	..	..	..	..
55 Mexico	12	10.4	8.2	9.2	15	9	28	14 c	3.6	58.2	16.2	17.9	10.1
56 Cuba	3	4.6	4.4	3.6	7	0	34	9	..	..	..	..	..
58 Belize	..	..	6	7.3	32	0	..	..	..	..	..	..	..
59 Panama	8	8.9	6.3	8.6	7	18	17	7	3.6	52.8	14.7	103	..
61 Malaysia	18	14	4.7	13.6	22	12	6	19	4.5	53.8	12.0	..	15.5
65 Venezuela	15	12.4	6.4	8	21	.. g	41	5	..	..	..	14.7	31.3
66 Fiji	6	8.4	4.9	7.8	23	1	8	8	..	..	..	..	..
67 Suriname	..	..	7.2	..	..	9	..	..	..	..	..	..	..
68 Colombia	11	10.4	9.8	8.8	15	13	15	8	3.0	60.9	20.3	11.0	17.7
71 Mauritius	14	11.6	4.8	16.2	2	1	0	16	..	..	..	..	10.6

(Contd.)

ANNEXURE TABLE 3 *(Contd.)*

1	*2*	*3*	*4*	*5*	*6*	*7*	*8*	*9*	*10*	*11*	*12*	*13*	*14*
72 Libyan Arab Jamhiriya	19	15.3	6.3	21.9	3	0	2	5	..	..	..	..	..
74 Brazil	21	15.6	11.3	15.5	24	.. g	30	6	2.5	63.8	25.5	5.1	17.4
75 Saudi Arabia	..	..	5.6	24.8	5 c	2	14	..	..	..	..	..	..
76 Thailand	29	18.7	10.4	5	19	41	4	19	6.4	48.4	7.6	28.2 e	13.1
77 Philippines	22	16.1	8.9	5.2	15	.. g	13	28	5.4	52.3	9.7	18.7 e	37.5
79 Saint Vincent and the Grenadines	..	..	..	..	11	20	2	..	..	..	..	..	..
80 Peru	25	16.5	11.3	10.8	33	.. g	28	8	4.4	51.2	11.6	15.5	49.0
High human development													
81 Paraguay	23	16.4	8.6	7.2	40	..g	59	4	2.3	62.4	27.1	19.4	21.8
82 Lebanon	13	10.8	7.3	14.9	6	5	37	3	..	..	..	..	..
83 Jamaica	16	13.4	5	14.0	14	..g	11	10	1.9	83.7	44.1	3.2	34.2
84 Sri Lanka	35	20.3	5.2	8.9	43	10	37	34	8.0	42.8	5.4	6.6	35.3
85 Turkey	24	16.4	9.3	16.0	51	0	20	10	5.8	47.7	8.2	2.4	..
86 Oman	38	22.7	6.2	31.2	15	11	22	23	..	..	..	..	..
87 Dominican Republic	20	15.4	8.8	17.2	21	..g	15	6	4.3	53.7	12.5	3.2	20.6
88 Saint Lucia	..	..	..	..	15	0	..	..	5.2	48.3	9.3	..	..
89 Maldives	43	25.4	13.0	4	40	25	56	43	..	..	..	..	..
91 Ecuador	26	16.8	10.9	9.4	32	20	24	17c	5.4	49.7	9.2	20.2	35.0
92 Jordan	7	8.8	6.9	11.4	3	10	1	5	7.6	44.4	5.8	7.4e	15.0
95 Somoa (Western)	..	..	5.3	20.3	32	0	..	..	..	..	..	..	..
96 Guyana	10	10.0	13.4	1.7	9	4	12	12	6.3	46.9	7.4	..	..

97 Iran. Islamic Rep. of	31	19.2	9.4	25.4	5	27	36	16	..	..	..	..	..
99 China	30	19.0	7.7	17.2	33	..g	76	16	5.9	46.6	7.9	..	6
101 Tunisia	36	21.9	7.5	31.3	2	10	20	9	5.9	46.3	7.8	1.3	19.9
103 South Africa	33	20.2	25.9	15.4	13	..g	13	9	2.9	64.8	22.3	11.5	..
104 El Salvador	34	20.2	10.7	22.2	34	..g	10	11	3.4	56.5	16.6	25.3	48.3
105 Cape Verde	37	22	10.1	27.1	35	18	73	14	..	..	..	..	..
107 Algeria	42	24.8	8.8	34.5	10	..g	9	13	7.0	42.6	6.1	15.1e	22.6
108 Viet Nam	47	28.2	11.2	7.1	55	..g	71	41	8.0	44.5	5.6	..	50.9
109 Indonesia	46	27.7	12.3	14.3	26	57	47	34	8.0	44.9	5.6	26.3	15.1
111 Syrian Arab Republic	32	19.3	8.2	27.3	14	1	33	13	..	..	..	..	..
112 Swaziland	45	27.4	20.2	21.7	50	45	41	10 C	2.7	64.4	23.9	..	..
113 Honduras	39	23.3	11.3	26.6	22	38	26	18	3.4	58.0	17.1	40.5	50.0
114 Bolivia	27	17.4	18.0	15.6	20	..g	35	10	5.6	48.2	8.6	11.3	..
115 Namibia	44	26.6	33.5	19.2	17	..g	38	26	..	..	..	34.9	..
116 Nicaragua	41	24.2	12.2	32.1	22	..g	15	12	4.2	55.2	13.1	3.0	50.3
117 Mongolia	..	..	10.9	..	32	0	..	..	7.3	40.9	5.6	..	..
118 Vanuatu	..	..	9.6	..	23	20	72	20 C	3.7	53.1	14.4	..	..
119 Eqypt	55	32.3	9.9	46.3	13	1	12	12	9.8	39.0	4.0	3.1	..
120 Guatemala	49	29.2	15.3	32.7	32	40	13	27	2.1	63.0	30.0	39.8	..
121 Solomon Islands	..	..	5.6	..	..	20	..	21 C	..	..	..	..	..
122 Botswana	48	28.3	37.1	24.4	10	14	45	17	..	..	..	33.3c	..
123 Gabon	..	..	30.7	..	33	13	..	..	..	..	..	..	..
124 Morocco	65	38.4	11.3	52.9	35	38	42	9	6.6	46.3	7	7.5e	26.0
125 Myanmar	53	31.4	17.6	15.9	40	52	57	39	..	..	..	..	..
126 Iraq	56	32.9	15.8	46.3	19	2	25	23	..	..	..	..	..

(Contd.)

ANNEXURE TABLE 3 *(Contd.)*

1	2	3	4	5	6	7	8	9	10	11	12	13	14
127 Lesotho	40	23.3	26.0	17.6	38	20	62	16	2.8	60.1	21.5	43.1	49.2
128 India	58	34.6	15.8	44.3	19	25	71	53	8.1	46.1	5.7	44.2	35.0
129 ghana	59	35.4	20.6	30.9	35	75	68	27	8.4	41.7	5.0	78.4	31.4
130 Zimbabwe	52	30.0	41.0	12.8	21	29	48	15	4.0	62.3	15.6	36	25.5
131 Equatorial Guinea	..	..	33.2	18.9	5	..	46	..	..	..	..	..	..
133 Sao Tome and Principe	..	..	..	..	18	12	65	16	..	..	..	..	..
133 Papua New Guinea	..	..	18.3	36.8	32	0	..	..	4.5	56.5	12.6	..	..
134 Cameroon	66	38.5	27.4	26.4	46	85	11	22	..	..	..	..	..
135 Pakistan	68	40.1	14.3	56.0	21	15	44	38	9.5	41.1	4.3	31.0	34.0
136 Cambodia	..	..	27.7	..	32	0	..	..	6.9	47.6	6.9	..	..
137 Comoros	57	33.0	20.1	41.5	47	18	77	26	..	..	..	..	..
138 Kenya	51	29.5	30.6	19.5	56	..g	15	22	5.0	50.2	10.0	26.5	42.0
139 Congo	54	31.9	34.4	21.6	66	..g	31	17c	..	..	..	..	..
Low human development													
140 Lao People's Dem. Rep.	..	..	28.9	53.9	32	0	..	..	9.6	40.2	4.2	..	..
141 Madagascar	..	..	21.8	35.1	32	0	..	..	5.1	52.1	10.2	..	..
142 Bhutan	..	..	19.6	..	42	20	30	38c	..	..	..	..	..
143 Sudan	60	35.5	26.6	44.3	27	30	49	34	..	..	..	..	..
144 Nepal	80	51.3	21.9	60.8	29	90	84	47	7.6	44.8	5.9	37.7	42.0
145 Togo	63	37.8	34.2	44.8	45	..g	63	25	..	..	..	..	32.3
146 Bangladesh	70	43.6	20.8	59.9	5	26	57	56	8.7	42.8	4.9	29.1	35.6

147 Mauritania	77	49.7	28.7	58.8	63	70	43	23	6.2	45.6	7.4	3.8	57.0
148 Yemen	76	49.4	21.2	55.9	39	84	34	46	6.1	46.1	7.6	5.1	19.1
149 Djibouti	..	..	32.8	37.7	32	0	..	..	..	..	..	..	..
150 Haiti	71	45.2	26.5	52.2	63	55	75	28	..	..	..	..	65.0
151 Nigeria	62	37.6	33.3	38.9	51	33	59	36	4.4	55.7	12.7	70.2	43
152 Congo, Dem. Rep. of the	..	..	31.7	41.1	32	0	..	..	..	..	..	..	..
153 Zambia	64	37.9	46.2	23.7	62	25	29	24	4.2	54.75	13.0	72.6	86.0
154 Cote d'Ivoire	72	45.8	370.0	55.5	58	40	61	24	7.1	44.3	6.2	12.3	..
155 Senegal	73	47.9	28.0	64.5	19	60	35	22	6.4	48.2	7.5	26.3	33.4
156 Tanzania, U. Rep. of	50	29.2	35.4	26.4	34	7	14	27	6.8	45.5	6.7	19.9	51.1
157 Benin	74	48.8	28.9	62.3	44	58	73	29	..	..	..	..	33.0
158 Uganda	67	39.7	45.9	35	54	29	43	26	6.6	46.1	7.0	36.7	55.0
159 Eritrea	..	..	31.4	48.3	32	0	..	..	..	..	..	..	..
160 Angola	..	..	37.7	..	69	76	60	42	..	..	..	..	..
161 Gambia	75	49.0	37.2	65.4	31	..g	63	26	4.4	52.8	12.0	53.7	64.0
162 Guinea	..	..	37.8	..	54	55	69	..	6.4	47.2	7.4	..	..
163 Malawi	69	41.9	47.5	41.8	53	20	97	30	..	..	..	..	54.0
164 Rwanda	61	37.5	45.9	36	21h	..g	..	27	9.7	39.1	4.0	35.7c	51.2
165 Mali	81	51.4	33.1	61.8	34	80	94	40	4.6	56.2	12.2	72.8	..
166 Central African Republic	82	53	40.4	56	62	88	73	27	2.0	65.0	32.5	66.6	..
167 Chad	..	..	36.9	60.6	32	0	..	..	..	..	..	..	..
168 Mozambique	79	50.7	41.9	57.7	54	70	66	26	6.5	46.5	7.2	37.9	..
169 Guinea-Bissau	78	50.2	40.6	63.3	57	36	54	23c	2.1	58.9	28.0	..	48.8

(Contd.)

Annexure Table 3 *(Contd.)*

1	2	3	4	5	6	7	8	9	10	11	12	13	14
170 Burundi	::	::	::	54.2	48	20	49	37	7.9	41.6	5.3	::	36.2
171 Ethiopia	83	55.3	42.1	63.7	75	45	81	48	7.1	47.7	6.7	31.3	::
172 Burkina Faso	84	58.4	39.9	77.8	58	30	63	30	5.5	55.0	10.0	61.2	::
173 Niger	85	64.7	35.2	85.3	39	70	81	50	2.6	53.3	20.5	61.4	63.0
174 Sierra Leone	::	::	50.0	::	66	64	89	29	1.1	63.4	57.6	57.0	68.0

Source: Human Development Report 2000

ANNEXURE TABLE 4

Poverty in India 1951-97 (with correction for CPIAL)

(Poverty line = Rs.49 per capita per month at Oct. 1973-Jun. 1974 rural prices)

NSS round	Survey Period	Headcount Index			Poverty Gap Index			Squared Poverty Gap Index		
		Rural	Urban	National	Rural	Urban	National	Rural	Urban	National
1	2	3	4	5	6	7	8	9	10	11
3	Aug. 1951-Nov. 1952	47.37	35.46	45.31	16.05	11.14	15.2	7.53	4.82	7.06
4	Apr. 1952-Sep. 1952	43.87	36.71	42.63	14.64	10.91	13.99	6.71	4.41	6.31
5	Dec. 1952-Mar. 1953	48.21	40.14	46.80	16.29	13.25	15.76	7.56	5.96	7.28
6	May 1953-Sep. 1953	54.13	42.77	52.15	19.03	13.83	18.12	9.12	6.29	8.62
7	Oct. 1953-Mar. 1954	61.29	49.92	59.30	21.95	17.24	21.12	10.26	7.74	9.82
8	Jul 1954-Mar. 1955	64.24	46.19	61.07	25.04	15.76	23.41	12.5	7.02	11.54
9	May 1955-Nov. 1955	51.83	43.92	50.44	18.44	14.65	17.78	8.80	6.40	8.38
10	Dec. 1955-May 1956	48.34	43.15	47.43	15.65	13.34	15.24	6.71	5.41	6.48
11	Aug. 1956-Feb. 1957	58.86	51.45	57.55	19.45	18.16	19.22	8.50	8.51	8.50
12	Mar. 1957-Aug. 1957	61.11	48.88	59.77	21.69	16.31	20.73	10.01	7.25	9.52
13	Sep. 1957-May 1958	55.16	47.75	53.84	19.01	15.95	18.47	8.78	7.00	8.46
14	Jul. 1958-Jan. 1959	53.26	44.76	51.75	17.74	13.75	17.03	7.88	5.87	7.52
15	Jul. 1959-Jan. 1960	50.89	49.17	50.58	15.29	15.83	15.39	6.13	6.75	6.24
16	Jul. 1960-Aug. 1961	45.40	44.65	45.27	13.6	13.84	13.64	5.33	5.83	5.59
17	Sep. 1961-Jul. 1962	47.20	43.55	46.54	13.6	13.79	13.64	5.31	6.05	5.45
18	Feb. 1963-Jan. 1964	48.53	44.83	47.85	13.88	13.29	13.77	5.49	5.17	5.43

(Contd.)

ANNEXURE TABLE 4 (Contd.)

1	2	3	4	5	6	7	8	9	10	11
19	Jul. 1964-Jun. 1965	53.66	48.78	52.75	16.08	15.24	15.93	6.60	6.38	6.56
20	Jul. 1965-Jun. 1966	57.6	52.9	56.71	17.97	16.82	17.75	7.60	6.98	7.49
21	Jul. 1966-Jun. 1967	64.3	52.24	62	22.01	16.81	21.02	10.01	7.19	9.47
22	Jul. 1967-Jun. 1968	63.67	52.91	61.6	21.8	16.93	20.86	9.85	7.22	9.35
23	Jul. 1968-Jun. 1969	59.0	49.29	57.11	18.96	15.54	18.29	8.17	6.54	7.85
24	Jul. 1969-Jun. 1970	57.61	47.16	55.56	18.24	14.32	17.47	7.73	5.86	7.36
25	Jul. 1970-Jun. 1971	54.84	44.98	52.88	16.55	13.35	15.91	6.80	5.35	6.51
27	Oct. 1972-Sep. 1973	55.36	45.67	53.37	17.35	13.46	16.55	7.33	5.26	6.90
28	Oct. 1973-Jun. 1974	55.72	47.96	54.1	17.18	13.60	16.43	7.13	5.22	6.73
32	Jul. 1977-Jun. 1978	50.6	40.5	48.36	15.03	11.69	14.28	6.06	4.53	5.72
38	Jan. 1983-Dec. 1983	45.31	35.65	43	12.65	9.52	11.9	4.84	3.56	4.53
42	Jul. 1986-Jun. 1987	38.81	34.29	37.69	10.01	9.10	9.79	3.70	3.40	3.63
43	Jul. 1987-Jun. 1988	39.23	36.2	38.47	9.28	9.12	7.24	2.98	3.06	3.00
44	Jul. 1988Jun. 1989	39.06	36.6	38.44	9.50	9.54	9.51	3.29	3.29	3.29
45	Jul. 1989-Jun. 1990	34.3	33.4	34.07	7.80	8.51	7.98	2.56	3.04	2.69
46	Jul. 1990-Jun. 1991	36.43	32.76	35.49	8.64	8.51	8.61	2.93	3.12	2.98
47	Jul. 1991-Dec. 1991	37.42	33.23	36.34	8.29	8.24	8.28	2.68	2.90	2.74
48	Jan. 1991-Dec. 1992	43.47	33.73	40.93	10.88	8.82	10.35	3.81	3.19	3.65
50	Jul. 1993-Jun. 1994	36.66	30.51	35.04	8.39	7.41	8.13	2.79	2.42	2.69
51	Jul. 1994-Jun. 1995	39.75	33.5	38.4	8.89	8.38	-	2.90	2.8	-
52	Jul. 1995-Jun. 1996	37.46	28.04	35	8.31	6.78	-	2.64	2.22	-
53	Jan. 1997-Dec. 1997	35.69	29.99	34.4	8.39	7.77	-	2.83	2.73	-

Source: World Bank, India-Reducing Poverty Accelerating Development, Oxford University Press, New Delhi, 2000.

ANNEXURE TABLE 5

State Poverty Rates

State	*Total*			*Rural*			*Urban*		
	HCI	*PGI*	*SPGI*	*HCI*	*PGI*	*SPGI*	*HCI*	*PGI*	*SPGI*
Punjab	11.46	1.84	0.46	11.69	1.90	0.48	10.90	1.69	0.40
Andhra Pradesh	21.87	4.54	1.48	15.89	2.88	0.86	38.82	9.27	3.20
Gujarat	24.15	4.77	1.42	22.16	4.07	1.16	28.28	6.22	1.96
Kerala	25.12	5.59	1.86	25.38	5.61	1.84	24.31	5.53	1.88
Haryana	25.22	4.94	1.51	28.26	5.60	1.74	16.47	3.05	0.85
Rajasthan	27.46	5.62	1.72	26.40	5.21	1.55	31.02	7.00	2.24
Himachal Pradesh	28.58	5.19	1.50	30.36	5.55	1.61	9.26	1.25	0.26
Karnataka	32.91	7.73	2.69	30.11	6.27	2.01	39.90	11.36	4.36
Tamil Nadu	35.40	8.33	3.00	32.95	7.30	2.49	39.92	10.23	3.92
Maharashtra	36.82	9.61	3.65	37.91	9.28	3.34	34.99	10.15	4.15
West Bengal	36.94	7.42	2.21	41.18	8.29	2.45	22.95	4.55	1.41
Assam	41.09	7.46	2.00	44.19	8.21	2.20	7.93	0.92	0.22
Uttar Pradesh	41.55	10.23	3.50	42.32	10.37	3.53	35.10	9.03	3.26
Madhya Pradesh	42.46	10.40	3.68	40.75	9.48	3.26	48.08	13.43	5.05
Orissa	48.64	11.89	4.10	49.81	11.96	4.07	40.64	11.41	4.29
Bihar	55.15	13.83	4.77	57.95	14.66	5.06	34.84	7.86	2.63
All India	36.13	8.42	2.86	37.07	8.43	2.80	33.06	8.38	3.07

Note: HCI : Headcount Index; PGI : Poverty Gap Index; SPGI : Squared Poverty Gap Index.

Source: World Bank, Reducing Poverty in India, Report No 1788-in, June 29, 1998.

ANNEXURE TABLE 6

Regional Poverty Rates

State	Total			Rural			Urban		
	HCI	PGI	SPGI	HCI	PGI	SPGI	HCI	PGI	SPGI
1	2	3	4	5	6	7	8	9	10
Andhra Pradesh Coast	24.05	5.14	1.72	17.07	3.23	1.00	43.45	10.46	3.60
Andhra Pradesh In Nth	18.22	3.39	1.00	13.92	2.25	0.60	30.60	6.69	2.10
Andhra Pradesh In Sth	20.75	4.54	1.44	12.97	2.17	0.50	44.62	11.83	4.20
Andhra Pradesh SW	26.92	6.20	2.25	20.85	4.35	1.40	43.07	11.17	4.30
Assam Hills	38.30	5.23	0.99	41.43	5.64	1.00	3.55	0.77	0.10
Assam Plains E	33.49	6.15	1.67	37.06	6.86	1.80	3.50	0.24	0.00
Assam Plains W	46.04	8.42	2.28	50.04	9.23	2.50	11.05	1.36	0.30
Bihar Cent	51.04	12.54	4.27	53.57	13.23	4.50	35.42	8.34	2.80
Bihar Nth	58.04	14.63	5.11	58.63	14.82	5.10	49.23	11.95	4.20
Bihar Sth (Jharkhand)	55.36	14.05	4.82	62.25	16.17	5.50	26.51	5.23	1.50
Gujarat Dry Areas	26.17	4.78	1.34	26.35	4.46	1.10	25.27	6.35	2.00
Gujarat East	26.32	5.51	1.59	25.54	5.41	1.50	33.90	6.57	1.80
Gujarat Plains Nth	25.80	4.93	1.43	23.31	3.84	0.90	29.17	6.41	2.00
Gujarat Plains Sth	23.75	5.22	1.69	26.19	5.31	1.50	20.16	5.09	1.80
Gujarat Saurastra	19.67	3.73	1.18	12.21	2.06	0.70	32.60	6.64	1.90
Haryana East	28.04	5.41	1.70	32.46	6.36	2.00	17.43	3.14	0.90
Haryana West	20.53	4.16	1.20	22.11	4.50	1.30	14.09	2.80	0.70
Himachal Pradesh	28.58	5.19	1.50	30.35	5.55	1.60	9.26	1.25	0.20

Karnataka Coast/Ghata	10.48	1.70	0.45	8.95	1.31	0.30	15.51	2.99	0.90
Karnataka Isle East	19.52	4.07	1.39	14.54	2.59	0.80	37.14	9.31	3.10
Karnataka Isle Nth	42.61	10.80	3.95	37.88	8.31	2.70	57.45	18.65	7.80
Karnatka Isle Sth	29.29	6.11	1.91	29.59	5.79	1.70	28.79	6.64	2.10
Kerala Nth	27.94	6.65	2.31	27.78	6.82	2.40	28.43	6.09	1.90
Kerala Sth	23.30	4.91	1.57	23.77	4.81	1.40	21.91	5.20	1.80
Madhya Pradesh Central	50.46	13.58	5.02	49.40	11.91	3.90	52.72	17.17	7.20
Madhya Pradesh Chattisgarh	44.39	9.09	2.75	44.42	8.58	2.40	44.24	11.52	4.00
Madhya Pradesh Malwa	33.51	7.41	2.39	27.83	5.52	1.60	45.51	11.40	3.80
Madhya Pradesh North	23.50	5.67	1.95	16.57	3.55	1.10	44.14	12.01	4.30
Madhya Pradesh Sth	47.64	12.61	4.61	46.43	11.80	4.20	50.71	14.69	5.50
Madhya Pradesh Sth/W	65.84	22.11	9.90	67.82	22.63	10.10	56.75	19.75	8.90
Madhya Pradesh Vindhya	38.70	8.33	2.57	36.72	7.70	2.30	50.85	12.25	3.90
Maharashtra Coast	13.31	2.41	0.67	15.22	2.50	0.60	12.45	2.37	0.60
Maharashtra East	49.80	10.91	3.54	49.30	10.66	3.40	52.72	12.38	4.30
Maharashtra Inland Cent	52.44	17.51	7.85	49.79	15.91	6.80	61.54	23.04	11.10
Maharashtra Inland East	52.61	14.49	5.46	49.11	11.49	3.60	59.03	20.02	8.70
Maharashtra Inland Nth	50.31	12.52	4.47	47.30	10.92	3.60	58.48	16.87	6.70
Maharashtra Inland W	29.30	6.40	2.19	24.92	5.00	1.60	40.17	9.90	3.60
Orisa Coast	45.57	10.67	3.47	45.33	10.33	3.31	47.23	13.07	4.50
Orissa Nth	43.95	10.20	3.49	45.87	10.55	3.54	32.45	8.15	3.10
Orissa Sth	66.07	18.46	6.99	68.84	18.86	7.06	41.94	15.06	6.30
Punjab Nth	7.64	1.10	0.27	7.32	1.07	0.26	8.32	1.16	0.20
Punjab Sth	16.96	2.89	0.73	17.41	2.98	0.77	15.60	2.65	0.60
Rajasthan NE	22.00	4.65	1.47	17.85	3.46	1.05	33.55	8.00	2.60

(Contd.)

ANNEXURE TABLE 6 (*Contd.*)

1	*2*	*3*	*4*	*5*	*6*	*7*	*8*	*9*	*10*
Rajasthan SE	35.86	8.52	2.81	33.94	7.92	2.56	42.76	10.68	3.70
Rajasthan Sth	44.11	9.33	2.79	46.30	9.77	2.89	26.59	5.89	1.90
Rajasthan W	24.86	4.26	1.18	25.32	4.27	1.19	23.33	4.26	1.10
Tamil Nadu Coast Nth	41.87	10.49	4.02	44.26	10.47	3.72	38.53	10.52	4.40
Tamil Nadu Coastal	26.05	5.58	1.90	20.80	4.01	1.32	43.00	10.69	3.70
Tamil Nadu Inland	25.54	4.76	1.38	22.15	3.94	1.13	32.02	6.32	1.80
Tamil Nadu South	40.97	10.22	3.71	37.20	8.72	3.05	48.36	13.18	5.00
Uttar Pradesh Central	48.29	13.28	4.84	50.23	13.78	5.01	33.85	9.52	3.50
Uttar Pradesh East	48.11	11.80	3.97	48.78	11.98	4.03	38.62	9.36	3.10
Uttar Pradesh Himal	23.56	4.25	1.06	24.83	4.36	1.08	12.66	3.25	0.80
Uttar Pradesh Sth	68.21	20.28	8.10	67.36	20.17	8.09	74.36	21.06	8.10
Uttar Pradesh West	29.55	6.32	1.98	29.29	6.08	1.85	31.12	7.74	2.70
West Bengal Cent Plains	26.29	5.45	1.70	31.41	6.74	2.10	18.23	3.43	1.00
West Bengal East	45.96	9.77	3.03	47.49	10.15	3.14	35.14	7.12	2.20
West Bengal Himal	55.51	11.10	3.10	58.42	11.56	3.19	32.62	7.48	2.40
West Bengal W plains	40.82	7.13	1.89	40.73	6.93	1.81	41.78	9.32	2.70

Source: World Bank, Reducing Poverty in India, Report No. 17881 -IN, June 29, 1998.

APPENDIX 1

An Empirical Study of Poverty Alleviation Programmes

Schedule for IRDP

1. **PLACE**

1.1 Zone

1.2 District

1.3 Block/Village panchayat

2. **IDENTIFICATION**

2.1 Beneficiary's Village

2.2 Beneficiary Category (See Code list)*

2.3 Name of the baneficiary

2.4 Sex (Male - 1, Female-2)

2.5 Size of the family of the beneficiary (number)

2.6 Beneficiary's occupation at the time of selection (see Code list)

2.7 Social Classification

(a) SC=1, ST=2, OBCs=3, Others=4

(b) Ex/freed Bonded labour =1,
Assignees of surplus land = 2
Physically hadicapped = 3,
Others = 4

2.8 (a) Literacy level (As per census Definition, Literate =1,Illiterate = 2)

(b) If literate, the level-(Primary & above-1, Matric & above-2, Graduation & above -3)

3. **SELECTION**

3.1 Annual Family income at the time of assistance

(a) As assessed by the Investigator

(b) As per record

3.2 Was he/she selected as a beneficiary in the Gram Sabha meeting (Assembly of Adult members)
(Yes =1, No =2)

3.3 If not, who selected him/her ? (See code List)

4. **PROVISION OF ASSET**

4.1 Whether Credit Camp was held for Completion of loan application formalities ? (Yes=1, No=2)

4.2 Date of receipt of application in block office
DD MM YY

4.3 Date of forwarding of loan application by the block to bank
DD MM YY

4.4 Date of sanction of loan by bank
DD MM YY

4.5 How many mandays (i.e. 8 hours = 1) did the beneficiary spend of visiting?

(a) Block Office
(b) Bank Office
(c) Other Offices
(d) Markets

4.6 How many days of wage employment the beneficiary had to forgo in visiting these offices ?
4.7 Actual wage rate per day at the time of survey.
4.8 How much money had he/she to spend on visits to block office/bank branch/other offices/ markets ?
4.9 Any other expenditure (Amount)
4.10 Sectoral Distribution of Assets
(i) Primary
(a) Agricultural
(b) Irrigation
(c) Milch Animal
(d) Animal Husbandry excluding primary milch animal
(ii) Secondary
(a) Handicraft
(b) Village industry
(iii) Tertiary
(a) Hotel
(b) Shops
(c) Tailoring

5. DETAILS OF THE BENEFITS RECIEVED

5.1 Whether the asset has been procured (Yes =1, No =2, Loan utilised for working capital and no asset required to be purchased = 3)
5.2 Actual cost of the scheme/asset
5.3 Amount of the unit cost fixed by NABARD
5.4 Cost of the scheme/asset in the opinion of the beneficiary
(Adequate -1, Inadequate -2, Inadequate due to exrtra expenditure-3)
5.5 Is the asset according to beneficiary's choice ? (Yes =1, No=2, NA=3)
5.6 What is the gestation period of the asset/scheme (in months)?
5.7 Gestation period prescribed by bank
5.8 Quality of the asset provided
(Good =1, Average = 2, poor=3, NA=4)
5.9 Whether the total amount of assistance received covered the entire cost of the asset/scheme ?
(Yes =1, No=2)
5.10 If not, how did the beneficiary manage the balance amount ? (Own sources =1, Borrowings =2)
5.11 If borrowed, what is the rate of interest (%) ?

6. DETAILS OF LOAN

6.1 Kind of financial Institution (See Code List)
6.2 Amount of loan disbursed

(a) As per record
(b) As verified from beneficiary

6.3 Amount of subsidy
6.4 Date of adjustment of subsidy
6.5 Rate of interest (%)
6.6 (a) Was any security/surety obtained for the loan ? (Yes =1, No =2)
(b) If yes, specify (property =1, Bond =2, Others =3)
6.7 Has loan pass-book been given to the beneficiary (Yes =1, No=2)
6.8 (a) Mode of repayment (See code List)
6.9 No. of instalments
6.10 Repayment period in months
6.11 Due date for repayment of 1st instalment
6.12 Is it before or after the gestation period ? (Before =1, After =2)
6.13 (a) No. of instalments paid so far
(b) Amount of instalment
(c) Total amount paid so far
(d) How was the loan repaid? (See Code List)
6.14 Is the beneficiary satisfied with the terms and conditions of the loan ? (Yes =1, No=2, Not aware =3)
6.15 If not, why ? (See Code List)
6.16 How much of the loan + Interest amount was due for repayment ?
6.17 How much loan was repaid so far ?
6.18 Amount of overdues
6.19 Reasons for overdues(See Code List)

7. CURRENT STATUS OF ASSETS

7.1 What is the current status of asset ? (Intact =1, Not intact =2)
7.2 If not intact, give status (As per Code list)
7.3 If asset not intact, reasons thereof (See Code List)

8. INSURANCE

8.1 (a) Whether the beneficiary was aware of the Group Life Insurance Scheme for IRDP beneficiary ? (Yes =1, No=2)
(b) Your asset is insured (Yes =1, No=2)

9. TRAINING

9.1 Whether any training was provided to beneficiary for handling the asset ?
(Yes =1, No=2, Not required =3)
9.2 If yes, Nature of training given (Formal =1, Informal =2, NA=3)
9.3 Utility of the training given (Useful =1, not useful =2, NA=3)
9.4 Scheme of Training

10. LINKAGES AND AFTER CARE

10.1 Does the beneficiary think that the existing infrastructure facilities in respect of the following are adequate ?
(a) Availability of inputs (Yes =1, No=2, Not required =3)
(b) Marketing of output/service (Yes =1, No =2)

(c) Availability of repair/maintenance service/other care (Yes =1, No =2)

10.2 What else is required to improve infrastructure facilities ?

10.3 Has the beneficiary been given continued support/guidance by Govt. Agencies on an on going basis ? (Yes = 1, No = 2 , Not Required = 3)

11. BENEFICIARY'S INDEBTEDNESS (ONLY IF OLD BENEFICIARY)

11.1 Whether beneficiary had any non-institutiional borrowing ?: (Yes = 1, No = 2)

11.2 If yes,

(a) Reasons there of (See Code List)

(b) Total amount borrowed

(c) Out of this, amount outstanding at present (including interest)

12. INCOME FROM ASSET/SCHEME (ONLY IF OLD BENEFICIARY)

12.1 Annual family income from asset/scheme

12.2 Total expenditure incurred on the maintenance of the asset/scheme during the preceeding 12 - months period

12.3 Total amount of loan repaid during the preceeding 12 - months period.

12.4 Net annual family income from the asset/scheme.

12.5 Net annual family income from other sources/previously existing sources including labour cost.

13.

13.1 What type of obstacles you have faced in getting IRDP loan ?

13.2 What are your broad suggestions for the improvement of IRDP scheme?

13.3 Do you have any information about the Group/Cluster beneficary's approach of IRDP ?

(Yes = 1, No = 2)

13.4 If yes, have you taken benefit of Group/Cluster beneficiary's approach of IRDP ?

(Yes = 1, No = 2)

14. Investigator's personal observation, if any

Date : Signature of the Investigator

Place :

CODE-LIST

Item 2.2

Beneficiary category Code	
1. New first dose	01
2. New second dose	02
3. Old first dose	03
4. Old second dose	04

Item 2.6

Occupation	Code
1. Small Farmer	01
2. Marginal Farmer	02
3. Agricultural Labour	03
4. Non-agricultural casual labour	04
5. Non-agricultural self-employed	05
6. Artisan	06
7. Others	07

Item 3.3

Sources Code	
1. Village Pradhan/Sarpanch/Panchayat Member	01
2. VLW	02
3. BDO/Other block officials (excluding VLW)	03
4. Panchayat Secretary	04
5. Co-Operative Secretary	05
6. DRDA Officials	06
7. Bank Officials	07
8. Fellow village/Neighbour	08
9. Village School Teacher	09
10. Patwari	10
11. MP/MLA/MLC	11
12. Land Lord/Employer Farmer	12
13. Own Effort	13
14. Others	14

Item 6.1

Financial Institution	Code
1. Commercial Bank	01
2. Regional Rural Bank	02
3. Co-operative Bank	03
4. Khadi & Village Industry Board	04
5. Khadi & Village Industry Commission	05

Item 6.8 Mode of Payment

1. Monthly	01
2. Quarterly	02
3. Biannual	03
4. Annual	04

Item 6.13 (d) How was the loan repaid ?

1. Through income generated from given assets	01

2.	By disposal of old assets	02
3.	Old Savings	03
4.	Borrowing from friends/relations	04
5.	Borrowing from money-lenders, traders, land lords	05
6.	No response	06

Item 6.15

1.	Interest Rate High	01
2.	Time Consuming Procedure	02
3.	Amount of loan/assistance is inadequate	03
4.	Capacity for repayment not taken into account	04
5.	Money demanded by officials and middlemen	05

6.19 Reasons for overdues

Asset perished	01
Delay in Income generation from the scheme	02
Inadequate income for regular payment	03
Lack of marketing facilities	04
Unfore seen calamity	05
Old Dues	06
Tight repayment Schedule	07
Others	08

Item 7.2 If not Intact Current Status

(a) Not purchases	01
(b) Sold	02
(c) Fully perished	03
(d) Defective	04
(e) Transferred without sale	05
(f) Others	06

Item 7.3 Reasons for not Intact

Unexpected contigency/personal natural calamities -	01
Not enough income was generated	02
Maintenance was costly	03
Defective	04
Cost of maintenance is higher because rise of prices of input required for maintenance	05
Cost of maintenance as anticipated, but it could not be afforded due to compulsive immediate household consumption requirements	06
Others	07

Item 11.2 (a) Reasons there of

Acquiring Asset under the scheme	01
Acquiring raw material under the scheme	02
Maintenance of unit under the scheme	03
Repayment of bank loan under the scheme	04
Household consumption	05
Repayment of Pre-IRDP loan	06
Other needs	07

Appendix 2

An Empirical Study of Poverty Alleviation Programmes Scheduled for TRYSEM

IDENTIFICATION

a. Zone
b. District
c. Block/Village Panchayat/Village
d. Name of the Beneficiary
e. Sex (Male-1, Female-2)
f. Age.
g. (i) Literacy Level (literate - 1, illiterate - 2)
(ii) If literate, the level (Primary & above -1, Matric & above -2, Graduation & above -3)
h. Beneficiary category - Small Farmer/Marginal Farmer/Agricultural Labour/Non-Agricultural
Casual Labour/Non-Agricultural Self-Employed/Artisan/Others
i. Social Classification
SC/ST/Ex/freed Bonded Labour/Assignees of surplus land/ Others
j. (a) Size of the family of beneficiary (number)
(b) Number of earning members in the beneficiary's family
k. Types of the beneficiary's family -
Nuclear/Joint
l. Income of the Household (Monthly)

Primary Occupation :		*Secondary Occupation :*		*Any other Sources :*	
Head	*Amount*	*Head*	*Amount*	*Head*	*Amount*

m. Annual family income of the Beneficiary

SELECTION

1. You had received the training in which year -
2. The course was of what duration -
3. You have been trained for which course -
4. Your opinion about the course
   (a) highly satisfactory
   (b) Satisfactory
   (c) Less satisfactory
   (d) Unsatisfactory
5. What was the reason of the unsatisfactory performance of the course
   (a) It was only a paper work
   (b) Trainers were not competent
   (c) There was no seriousness about the course
   (d) You got engaged in some other works

6. Could you develop skill in the training area ? - Yes/No
7. How had you been selected for training ? -
   (i) On the basis of merit test
   (ii) Help of block authority
   (iii) Help of panchayat authority
   (iv) Help of influencial persons
   (v) Easy access due to mass unawareness about the scheme
8. (i) What was the stipend amount for the course
   (ii) Had you received the stipend amount
      (i) totally
      (ii) Partially
9. In case of partial payment which one got the rest amount
   (i) Block authority
   (ii) Middle man
   (iii) No idea
10. Did you get any benefit from the training -
   (i) New job assignment
   (ii) Enhancement in the productivity level under self employment
   (iii) Enhancement in the quality level under self employment
   (iv) Receiving loan for any project under self employment scheme
   (v) No benefit
11. (i) Did you receive IRDP loan on the basis of Training - Yes/No
   (ii) If No, what was the reason
   (a) You have not applied
   (b) You have applied but could not get due to procedural obstacles/ corruption
   (c) Any other, specify
12. (i) Are you engaged in the same activity in which you had received training - Yes/No
   (ii) If yes, your income level has been raised due to training - Yes/No
   (iii) If no, specify reasons -
13. You are working in
   (a) Self employment scheme
   (b) Wage employment scheme

GENERAL

(a) Beneficiary's observation about TRYSEM

(b) Investigator's observation

Date : Signature of Investigator

Place :

APPENDIX 3

An Empirical Study of Poverty Alleviation Programmes Scheduled for DWCRA

IDENTIFICATION

a. Zone

b. District

c. Block/Village Panchayat/Village

d. Name of the Beneficiary

e. Sex (Male-1, Female-2)

f. Age.

g. (i) Literacy Level (literate - 1, illiterate - 2)

(ii) If literate, the level (Primary & above -1, Matric & above -2, Graduation & above -3)

h. Beneficiary category - Small Farmer/Marginal Farmer/Agricultural Labour/Non-Agricultural
Casual Labour/Non-Agricultural Self-Employed/Artisan/Others

i. Social Classification
SC/ST/Ex/freed Bonded Labour/Assignees of surplus land/ Others

j. (a) Size of the family of beneficiary (number)

(b) Number of earning members in the beneficiary's family

k. Types of the beneficiary's family -
Nuclear/Joint

l. Income of the Household (Monthly)

Primary Occupation :		*Secondary Occupation :*		*Any other Sources :*	
Head	*Amount*	*Head*	*Amount*	*Head*	*Amount*

m. Annual family income of the Beneficiary

SELECTION

1. You had received the training in which year -
2. The course was of what duration -
3. You have been trained for which course -
4. Your opinion about the course
   (a) highly satisfactory
   (b) Satisfactory
   (c) Less satisfactory
   (d) Unsatisfactory
5. What was the reason of the unsatisfactory performance of the course
   (a) It was only a paper work
   (b) Trainers were not competent
   (c) There was no seriousness about the course
   (d) You got engaged in some other works

6. Could you develop skill in the training area ? - Yes/No
7. How had you been selected for training ? -
   (i) On the basis of merit test
   (ii) Help of block authority
   (iii) Help of panchayat authority
   (iv) Help of influencial persons
   (v) Easy access due to mass unawareness about the scheme
8. (i) What was the stipend amount for the course
   (ii) Had you received the stipend amount
      (i) totally
      (ii) Partially
9. In case of partial payment which one got the rest amount
   (i) Block authority
   (ii) Middle man
   (iii) No idea
10. Did you get any benefit from the training -
   (i) New job assignment
   (ii) Enhancement in the productivity level under self employment
   (iii) Enhancement in the quality level under self employment
   (iv) Receiving loan for any project under self employment scheme
   (v) No benefit
11. (i) Did you receive IRDP loan on the basis of Training - Yes/No
   (ii) If No, what was the reason
   (a) You have not applied
   (b) You have applied but could not get due to procedural obstacles/corruption
   (c) Any other, specify
12. (i) Are you engaged in the same activity in which you had received training - Yes/No
   (ii) If yes, your income level has been raised due to training - Yes/No
   (iii) If no, specify reasons -
13. You are working in
   (a) Self employment scheme
   (b) Wage employment scheme

GENERAL

(a) Beneficiary's observation about DWCRA

(b) Investigator's observation

Date : Signature of Investigator

Place :

APPENDIX 4

An Empirical Study of Poverty Alleviation Programmes Scheduled for JRY

IDENTIFICATION

a. Zone
b. District
c. Block/Village Panchayat/Village
d. Name of the Beneficiary
e. Sex (Male-1, Female-2)
f. (i) Literacy Level (literate - 1, illiterate - 2)
(ii) If literate, the level (Primary & above -1, Matric & above -2, Graduation & above -3)
g. Beneficiary category - Small Farmer/Marginal Farmer/Agricultural Labour/Non-Agricultural
Casual Labour/Non-Agricultural Self-Employed/Artisan/Others
h. Social Classification
SC/ST/Ex/freed Bonded Labour/Assignees of surplus land/ Others
i. (a) Size of the family of beneficiary (number)
(b) Number of earning members in the beneficiary's family
j. Types of the beneficiaries family -
Nuclear/Joint

SELECTION

a. Income of the Household (Monthly)
Primary Occupation : Secondary Occupation :
Any other Sources :
Head *Amount*
Head *Amount*
Head *Amount*

b. Annual family income of the Beneficiary
c. Method of selection of works under JRY
On the recommendations of :
i. Gram Sabha
ii. Panchayat
iii. Block Officials
iv. NGO
v. Influencial persons
d. Source of information of JRYworks
i. BDO
ii. Panchayat
iii. VLW

iv. Friends
v. NGO
vi. Contractor
vii. Any other, specify
e. Selection of workers on the recommendations of :
i. Gram Sabha
ii. Sarpanch
iii. VLW
iv. BDO
v. NGO
vi. Influencial persons
vii. Contractor
viii. Any other, specify
f. Selection of works based on the felt needs of people - Yes/No
g. How did you get employment on JRY works ?
i. By paying some money
ii. By doing the work for some one
iii. Proximity with the contractor
iv. Any other, specify
h. Did you possess some special skill? - Yes/No
i. Was the work available?
(a) Within the village
(b) Outside the village
j. Nature of facilities extended to work site of JRY
i. Rest shelters
ii. Drinking water
iii. Creches
iv. Others, specify
v. No facility

EXECUTION OF WORKS

a. Who executed the works?
i. Contractors
ii. PRIs
iii. Department
iv. NGO
v. Any other, specify
b. Works executed in the area
i. Inhabited predominantly by SC/ST
ii. Concealed bonded labour
iii. Low wage pocket area
iv. Randomly selected

WAGES UNDER JRY

a. Wage rate
i. At par with local rate
ii. Below local rate
iii. Higher than local rate
b. Are you aware of minimum wage rate? - Yes/No
c. Whether minimum wage rate is paid? - Yes/No/No Knowledge
d. If wages are not higher than local rate, why did you offer to take employment in JRY works?
i. Easy work
ii. Available in lean Agricultural season/Non availability of work
iii. Closer to home
iv. Any other, specify
e. Any difference between the wages of
i. Men/Women - Yes/No
ii. Skilled and unskilled work - Yes/No
f. Mode of payment of wages
i. Daily
ii. Weekly
iii. Fortnightly
iv. Monthly
v. No fixed period
g. System of payment of wages
i. Time bias
ii. Piece rated

EMPLOYMENT UNDER JRY

a. How many schemes of JRY did you work in ?
i. One
ii. Two
iii. Three
iv. More
b. Besides JRY, has any other member of your family or have you got benefitted from Rural Development Programme? - Yes/No
c. If yes, name the scheme
d. Total No. of days worked under JRY in a year
No. of days -

	Scheme					
	I	*II*	*III*	*IV*	*V*	*Total*
i. Less than 10 days						
ii. 10-15 days						
iii. 16-20 days						
iv. 21-30 days						
v. 31-40 days						

vi. 41-60 days
vii. More than 60 days

ASSETS GENERATED UNDER JRY

a. Nature of assets created -
i. Durable, specify
ii. Non-durable, specify
b. i. Useful
ii. Wasteful
c. If useful, to whom they are useful -
i. Community as a whole
ii. Weaker Sections
iii. Better-off sections
iv. Vested interests
d. Have the assets improved the production potential of the area? - Yes/No
e. Has the Social infrastructure i.e. School Building
i. Improved Enrolment of children in the school?
ii. Reduced drop-outs?
iii. Improved educational standard?
iv. No impact?
v. No work has been done for school building under JRY?
f. Creation of Panchayat Ghars/Community Centre led to
i. More interaction and communication among people, social and political
ii. Greater awareness among people
iii. Greater health care hygiene etc.
iv. No use due to different factor
(a) Distance
(b) Location
(c) Other, specify
v. Resource wastefulness

GENERAL AWARENESS ABOUT

a. Do you find the programme to be useful? - Yes/No
b. Has it improved your income level? - Yes/No
c. If yes, is the improvement
i. Marginal
ii. Significant
iii. Average
d. Has it led to improvement in? -
i. Nutritional needs
ii. Education of child
iii. Social functions

iv. Savings
v. Clothings
vi. Better House
vii. Maintaining household consumption expenditure
viii. Any other, specify

GENERAL

(a) Beneficiary's observation about JRY

(b) Investigator's observation

Date : Signature of the Investigator
Place :

Appendix 5

An Empirical Study of Poverty Alleviation Programmes Scheduled for EAS

IDENTIFICATION

a. Zone
b. District
c. Block/Village Panchayat/Village
d. Name of the Beneficiary
e. Sex (Male-1, Female-2)
f. (i) Literacy Level (literate - 1, illiterate - 2)
(ii) If literate, the level (Primary & above -1, Matric & above -2, Graduation & above -3)
g. Beneficiary category - Small Farmer/Marginal Farmer/Agricultural Labour/Non-Agricultural
Casual Labour/Non-Agricultural Self-Employed/Artisan/Others
h. Social Classification
SC/ST/Ex/freed Bonded Labour/Assignees of surplus land/ Others
i. (a) Size of the family of beneficiary (number)
(b) Number of earning members in the beneficiary's family
j. Types of the beneficiaries family -
Nuclear/Joint

SELECTION

a. Income of the Household (Monthly)
Primary Occupation : Secondary Occupation :
Any other Sources :

Head	*Amount*
Head	*Amount*
Head	*Amount*

b. Annual family income of the Beneficiary
c. Method of selection of works under EAS
On the recommendations of :
i. Gram Sabha
ii. Panchayat
iii. Block Officials
iv. NGO
v. Influencial persons
d. Source of information of EASworks
i. BDO
ii. Panchayat
iii. VLW

iv. Friends
v. NGO
vi. Contractor
vii. Any other, specify
e. Selection of workers on the recommendations of :
i. Gram Sabha
ii. Sarpanch
iii. VLW
iv. BDO
v. NGO
vi. Influencial persons
vii. Contractor
viii. Any other, specify
f. Selection of works based on the felt needs of people - Yes/No
g. How did you get employment on EAS works ?
i. By paying some money
ii. By doing the work for some one
iii. Proximity with the contractor
iv. Any other, specify
h. Did you possess some special skill? - Yes/No
i. Was the work available?
(a) Within the village
(b) Outside the village
j. Nature of facilities extended to work site of EAS
i. Rest shelters
ii. Drinking water
iii. Creches
iv. Others, specify
v. No facility

EXECUTION OF WORKS

a. Who executed the works?
i. Contractors
ii. PRIs
iii. Department
iv. NGO
v. Any other, specify
b. Works executed in the area
i. Inhabited predominantly by SC/ST
ii. Concealed bonded labour
iii. Low wage pocket area
iv. Randomly selected

WAGES UNDER EAS

a. Wage rate
i. At par with local rate
ii. Below local rate
iii. Higher than local rate
b. Are you aware of minimum wage rate? - Yes/No
c. Whether minimum wage rate is paid? - Yes/No/No Knowledge
d. If wages are not higher than local rate, why did you offer to take employment in EAS works?
i. Easy work
ii. Available in lean Agricultural season/Non availability of work
iii. Closer to home
iv. Any other, specify
e. Any difference between the wages of
i. Men/Women - Yes/No
ii. Skilled and unskilled work - Yes/No
f. Mode of payment of wages
i. Daily
ii. Weekly
iii. Fortnightly
iv. Monthly
v. No fixed period
g. System of payment of wages
i. Time bias
ii. Piece rated

EMPLOYMENT UNDER EAS

a. How many schemes of EAS did you work in ?
i. One
ii. Two
iii. Three
iv. More
b. Besides EAS, has any other member of your family or have you got benefitted from Rural Development Programme? - Yes/No
c. If yes, name the scheme
d. Total No. of days worked under EAS in a year
No. of days -

	Scheme					
	I	*II*	*III*	*IV*	*V*	*Total*
i. Less than 10 days						
ii. 10-15 days						
iii. 16-20 days						
iv. 21-30 days						

v. 31-40 days
vi. 41-60 days
vii. More than 60 days

ASSETS GENERATED UNDER EAS

a. Nature of assets created -
i. Durable, specify
ii. Non-durable, specify
b. i. Useful
ii. Wasteful
c. If useful, to whom they are useful -
i. Community as a whole
ii. Weaker Sections
iii. Better-off sections
iv. Vested interests
d. Have the assets improved the production potential of the area? - Yes/No
e. Has the Social infrastructure i.e. School Building
i. Improved Enrolment of children in the school?
ii. Reduced drop-outs?
iii. Improved educational standard?
iv. No impact?
v. No work has been done for school building under EAS?
f. Creation of Panchayat Ghars/Community Centre led to
i. More interaction and communication among people, social and political
ii. Greater awareness among people
iii. Greater health care hygiene etc.
iv. No use due to different factor
(a) Distance
(b) Location
(c) Other, specify
v. Resource wastefulness

GENERAL AWARENESS ABOUT

a. Do you find the programme to be useful? - Yes/No
b. Has it improved your income level? - Yes/No
c. If yes, is the improvement
i. Marginal
ii. Significant
iii. Average
d. Has it led to improvement in? -
i. Nutritional needs
ii. Education of child

iii. Social functions
iv. Savings
v. Clothings
vi. Better House
vii. Maintaining household consumption expenditure
viii. Any other, specify

GENERAL

(a) Beneficiary's observation about EAS

(b) Investigator's observation

Date : Signature of the Investigator
Place :

Appendix 6

An Empirical Study of Poverty Alleviation Programmes

Scheduled of Indira Awas Yojana (IAY)

IDENTIFICATION

a. Zone

b. District

c. Block/Village Panchayat/Village

d. Name of the Beneficiary

e. Sex (Male-1, Female-2)

f. Age.

g. (i) Literacy Level (literate - 1, illiterate - 2)

(ii) If literate, the level (Primary & above -1, Matric & above -2, Graduation & above -3)

h. Beneficiary category - Small Farmer/Marginal Farmer/Agricultural Labour/Non-Agricultural
Casual Labour/Non-Agricultural Self-Employed/Artisan/Others

i. Social Classification
SC/ST/Ex/freed Bonded Labour/Assignees of surplus land/ Others

j. (a) Size of the family of beneficiary (number)

(b) Number of earning members in the beneficiary's family

k. Types of the beneficiary's family -
Nuclear/Joint

l. Income of the Household (Monthly)

Primary Occupation :		*Secondary Occupation :*		*Any other Sources :*	
Head	*Amount*	*Head*	*Amount*	*Head*	*Amount*

m. Annual family income of the Beneficiary

SELECTION

1. You have received the IAY help for which purpose
   (a) Repairing of house
   (b) Construction of house
2. What was the amount ?
3. Who did the construction/repairing work? -
   (a) Yourself (b) Contractor (c) Block authority (d) Panchayat authority
   (e) Any other, specify
4. (i) Are you satisfied with the construction/repairing work? - Yes/No
   (ii) If no, why -
   (a) Amount was not adequate
   (b) A portion of sanctioned amount taken by concerned authority
   (c) Any other, specify

5. (i) Have you paid any amount for inclusion of your land in IAY scheme ? - Yes/No
   (ii) If yes, who had taken the amount
   (a) Panchayat authority
   (b) Block authority
   (c) Middle man
6. (i) Better housing facility would help you in raising the income level - Yes/No
   (ii) If no, why
   (a) There is no major change in living standard
   (b) Other conditions are the same
   (c) Any other, specify

General

(a) Beneficiary's observation about IAY

(b) Investigator's observation

Date :

Place :

Signature of the Investigator

Appendix 7

An Empirical Study of Poverty Alleviation Programmes

Scheduled of National Old Age Pension Scheme (NOAPS)

IDENTIFICATION

a. Zone

b. District

c. Block/Village Panchayat/Village

d. Name of the Beneficiary

e. Sex (Male-1, Female-2)

f. Age.

g. (i) Literacy Level (literate - 1, illiterate - 2)

(ii) If literate, the level (Primary & above -1, Matric & above -2, Graduation & above -3)

h. Beneficiary category - Small Farmer/Marginal Farmer/Agricultural Labour/Non-Agricultural
Casual Labour/Non-Agricultural Self-Employed/Artisan/Others

i. Social Classification
SC/ST/Ex/freed Bonded Labour/Assignees of surplus land/ Others

j. (a) Size of the family of beneficiary (number)

(b) Number of earning members in the beneficiary's family

k. Types of the beneficiary's family -
Nuclear/Joint

l. Income of the Household (Monthly)

Primary Occupation :		*Secondary Occupation :*		*Any other Sources :*	
Head	*Amount*	*Head*	*Amount*	*Head*	*Amount*

m. Annual family income of the Beneficiary

SELECTION

1. You are receiving the pension from which year-
2. The pension amount per month -
3. The mode of payment -
   (a) Monthly
   (b) Quarterly
   (c) Half-Yearly
   (d) Yearly
   (e) No fixed period
4. (i) Did you received the amount in full ? - Yes/No
   (ii) If no, mention the actual amount received by you -
5. (i) Had you paid any amount for inclusion of your name in the pensioner list ? - Yes/No
   (ii) If yes, What is the amount

(iii) Who had taken the amount
(a) Block authority
(b) Panchayat authority
(c) Middle man

6. (i) Whether you used the amount for your own purpose- Yes/No
(ii) If no, mention the purpose
(a) for family
(b) for loan repayment
(c) any other, specify

General

(a) Beneficiary's observation about NOAPS

(b) Investigator's observation

Date : Signature of the Investigator
Place :

APPENDIX 8

An Empirical Study of Poverty Alleviation Programmes

Scheduled of National Maternity Benefit Scheme (NMBS)

IDENTIFICATION

a. Zone

b. District

c. Block/Village Panchayat/Village

d. Name of the Beneficiary

e. Sex (Male-1, Female-2)

f. Age.

g. (i) Literacy Level (literate - 1, illiterate - 2)

(ii) If literate, the level (Primary & above -1, Matric & above -2, Graduation & above -3)

h. Beneficiary category - Small Farmer/Marginal Farmer/Agricultural Labour/Non-Agricultural
Casual Labour/Non-Agricultural Self-Employed/Artisan/Others

i. Social Classification
SC/ST/Ex/freed Bonded Labour/Assignees of surplus land/ Others

j. (a) Size of the family of beneficiary (number)

(b) Number of earning members in the beneficiary's family

k. Types of the beneficiary's family -
Nuclear/Joint

l. Income of the Household (Monthly)

Primary Occupation :		*Secondary Occupation :*		*Any other Sources :*	
Head	*Amount*	*Head*	*Amount*	*Head*	*Amount*

m. Annual family income of the Beneficiary

SELECTION

1. How much amount you have received under the scheme : -
2. Source of payment -
   (i) Block office
   (ii) Panchayat office
   (iii) Health centre
   (iv) Any other, specify
3. Time taken by the authority in payment after filing the application -
4. You have received the amount during pre-natal or post-natal maternity period -
5. (i) Have you paid any amount for getting the benefit ? Yes/No
   (ii) If yes, mention the amount paid -
   (iii) Who has taken the amount ?
   (a) panchayat authority

(b) Block authority
(c) Any other, specify

6. (i) Whether the amount paid was used for required purpose ? - Yes/No
(ii) If no, why -
(a) Due to poverty and consumption requirement of the family
(b) Due to loan repayment
(c) Any other, specify
7. Do you feel the amount as adequate - Yes/No
If no, mention the adequate amount is Rs......................
8. Total number of children (Classify sex wise) -
Male Female Total
(i) In case of only female child/children, is there any preference for a male child - Yes/No/No Opinion/NA
9. (i) Did you receive the assistance under this scheme, prior to this - Yes/No
(ii) If yes, how many times

GENERAL

(a) Beneficiary's observation about NFBS

(b) Investigator's observation

Date :
Place :

Signature of Investigator

Appendix 9

An Empirical Study of Poverty Alleviation Programmes

Scheduled of National Family Benefit Scheme (NFBS)

IDENTIFICATION

a. Zone
b. District
c. Block/Village Panchayat/Village
d. Name of the Beneficiary
e. Sex (Male-1, Female-2)
f. Age.
g. (i) Literacy Level (literate - 1, illiterate - 2)
   (ii) If literate, the level (Primary & above -1, Matric & above -2, Graduation & above -3)
h. Beneficiary category - Small Farmer/Marginal Farmer/Agricultural Labour/Non-Agricultural
   Casual Labour/Non-Agricultural Self-Employed/Artisan/Others
i. Social Classification
   SC/ST/Ex/freed Bonded Labour/Assignees of surplus land/ Others
j. (a) Size of the family of beneficiary (number)
   (b) Number of earning members in the beneficiary's family
k. Types of the beneficiary's family -
   Nuclear/Joint
l. Income of the Household (Monthly)

Primary Occupation :		*Secondary Occupation :*		*Any other Sources :*	
Head	*Amount*	*Head*	*Amount*	*Head*	*Amount*

m. Annual family income of the Beneficiary

SELECTION

1. What was your relation with the deceased ?
2. When did he die?
3. When did you receive the amount ?
4. (i) Have you paid any amount to the block authority for recommendation ? - Yes/No
   (ii) If yes, What was the amount ?
5. (i) Had you paid any amount for sanction of the amount from district authority?- Yes/No
   (ii) If yes, What was the amount ?
   (iii) Who had taken the amount?
   (a) Directly the office
   (b) Middle man
   (c) Any other, specify

6. How did you utilise the amount ? -
   (a) On consumption expenditure
   (b) Undertaken an productive activity
   (c) Repayment of loan
   (d) Any other, specify

GENERAL

(a) Beneficiary's observation about NFBS

(b) Investigator's observation

Date : Signature of the Investigator
Place :

BIBLIOGRAPHY

Amarendra, 1998, Poverty, Rural Development and Public Policy, Deep & Deep Publication Pvt. Ltd., New Delhi.

Chakravarty, Sukhamoy, 1989.

Development Planning the Indian Experience. Oxford University Press, Delhi.

Dreze, Jean & Sen, Amartya, 1998, Indian Development Seleted Regional Perspectives.

———, 1998, India-Economic Development and Social Opportunity, Oxford University Press, New Delhi.

Government of India, 1999.

Economic Survey, 1998-99, Ministry of Finance, Economic Division.

Government of India, 2000, Economic Survey, 1999-2000. Ministry of Finance, New Delhi.

Haq, Mahbub Ul, 2000, Reflections on Human Development. Oxford University Press, New Delhi.

Joshi, Vijay Little, I.M.D. 1999. India's Economic Reforms, 1991-2001, Oxford India Paperbacks, Oxford University Press, New Delhi.

Murthy, Ranjani K., Rao, Nitya, 1997, Addressing Poverty, Friedrich Ebert Stiftung (India Office), New Delhi.

Nurkse, Ragnar, 1974, Problems of Capital Formation in Underdeveloped Countries, Oxford University Press, Delhi.

Parikh, Kirit S., 1999, India Development Report, 1999-2000. Oxford University Press, New Delhi.

Planning Commission, 1978, Draft Five Year Plan, 1978-83, Government of India, New Delhi.

———, 1981, Sixth Five Year Plan, 1980-85, Government of India, New Delhi.

Planning Commission, 1981, A Technical Note on the Sixth Plan of India, 1980-85, Government of India, New Delhi.

———, 1985, Seventh Five Year Plan Vols. I & II, 1985-90, Government of India, New Delhi.

———, 1986, A Technical Note on the Seventh Plan of India, 1985-90, New Delhi.

———, 1992, Eighth Five Year Plan, Vols. I & II, 1992-97, Government of India, New Delhi.

———, 1993, Report of the Expert Group on Estimation of Proportion and Number of Poor.

——— 1995, A Technical Note to the Eighth Plan of India 1992-97, Government of India, New Delhi.

———, 1997, Ninth Five Year Plan, Vols. I & II, 1997-2002, Government of India, Planning Commission, New Delhi.

Reserve Bank of India, 1997. Occasional Papers, Vol. 18, Nos. 2 & 3, Reserve Bank of India, Mumbai.

——— 2000, Bulletin—August, September, October, Mumbai.

SAARC, 1992, Meeting the Challenge, Report of the Independent South Asian Commission on Poverty Alleviation, SAARC Secretariat, Kathmandu.

Sen, Amartya, 1987, Poverty and Famines—An Essay on Entitlement and Deprivation, Oxford University Press, Oxford Ox26dp.

———, 1992, Inequality Reexamined, Oxford University Press, Oxford Ox26dp.

Sharif, Abusaleh, 1999, India: Human Development Report NCAER, Oxford University Press, New Delhi.

Sinha, Ajit Kumar, Sen, Raj Kumar, 2000, Economics of Amartya Sen, Deep & Deep Publications Pvt. Ltd., New Delhi.

Srinivasan, T.N., 2000, Eight Lectures on India's Economic Reforms, Oxford University Press, New Delhi.

UNDP, 2000, Human Development Report, 2000. Oxford University Press, New Delhi.

The World Bank, 1990, World Development Report—Poverty—Oxford University Press, Washington, D.C., USA.

———, 1998, Reducing Poverty in India: Options for More Effective Public Services, Report No. 17881, in, Washington, D.C.

———, 2000, World Development Report, 2000/2001, Attacking Poverty, Oxfoed University Press, New York.

The World Bank, 2000, India Reducing Poverty, Accelarating Development, Oxford University Press, New Delhi.

———, 2000, India Policies to Reduce Poverty and Accelerate Sustainable Development, Report No. 19471, in Washington, D.C., USA.

INDEX

T

U

W